BURMA 1942

MEMORIES OF A RETREAT

R.E.S. TANNER AND D.A. TANNER

BURMA 1942

MEMORIES OF A RETREAT

THE DIARY OF RALPH TANNER, KOYLI

The History Press

Dedicated to the memory of Corporal James Hart 4688955, who stayed behind at Bilin on 19th February 1942 to care for a wounded friend, and was never seen again.

Cover illustration: The final river crossing, the Chindwin at Yuwa, 14 May.

First published 2009
This paperback edition published 2019

The History Press
97 St George's Place, Cheltenham,
Gloucestershire, GL50 3QB
www.thehistorypress.co.uk

British Library Cataloguing in Publication Data.
A catalogue record for this book is available from the British Library.

ISBN 978 0 7509 9236 7

Typesetting and origination by The History Press
Printed and bound in Great Britain by TJ International Ltd

MIX
Paper from responsible sources
FSC® C013056

Contents

Remembering a damaged man

Dr Ralph Tanner died in 2017. Ralph and David Tanner stated in the foreword that this was not a personal memoir, but it is only because of the personal nature of both his diary, discussions and notes for this book that we have had this insight into the tragedy. Burma was never far from Ralph's thoughts up until his death. In 1942 a young man was transported instantly into adulthood and saw death, stupidity and bravery, and came to respect his enemy as an efficient fighting force. He escaped to India as, in his own words, a physically and mentally damaged man. As part of what would become an ongoing Burma nexus, he returned to Burma in 1946 with his young wife and son, David, to assist the country in extracting itself from British colonial rule. In later years, whether it was philately or his wife's paintings, Burma remained a focus.

Acknowledgements

The authors wish to express their thanks to the Regimental Museum of the 2nd Battalion The Kings Own Yorkshire Light Infantry at Doncaster for their permission to publish photograph numbers 2, 3, 4, 5, 6, 7, 8, 9, 10 and 11. All other photographs are from the authors' private collection or from the History Press archives. Maps shown as Appendix C and C1 are reproduced from the abridged Japanese regimental history of the 214 and 215 Regiments covering the actions in 1942. It has not been possible to locate the copyright holders of this privately published material. The Authors and Publishers would be most grateful for any information and will undertake to credit any parties identified on reprint.

The authors would also like to thank Kazuo Sawa for his research that located the officers of the Japanese 33 Division, Meredith Harte and Todd Londagin for their help in sourcing aircraft photographs, Reiko Fukushima for her help with some of the Japanese translations, and The Royal Geographical Society for the provision of maps to which the authors did not have access. (It is impossible to reproduce old maps with perfect clarity in a book of this size – though Ralph Tanner's own sketch maps are perfectly understandable – but the others reproduced here are artefacts that act in themselves as conduits of memory, at least to those who fought and marched across their pages; for this reason if no other they have been included.

Annotations of the movements of KOYLI and other details have been added to them.)

A great debt of thanks is owed to John Heald and the Regimental Museum for Appendix D.

Lastly, thanks are due to Malcolm Johnson, the unofficial historian of the 2nd Battalion The Kings Own Yorkshire Light Infantry for his encouragement and suggestions after reading the first draft of this work.

Foreword

This is a study of a tragedy. It does not seek to accuse but to investigate, and to highlight the extraordinary bravery of those who survived and those who did not. It is an assessment of the work undertaken by the Second Battalion of the King's Own Yorkshire Light Infantry from the time of their mobilisation in August 1941 until they reached India at the end of May 1942 as an exhausted remainder after 164 days of fighting, disasters and deprivation. It is not simply a personal memoir, although Ralph Tanner, in the second half of the campaign, as a newly commissioned Second Lieutenant, wrote a diary within twelve months after his arrival in India, which forms the basis of this book, together with maps that he kept on his person throughout the retreat, shown in Appendix A. The diary has been supported by maps from other sources and diagrams, along with photographs which he had taken.

Burma 1942 addresses the shortcomings of memory within the context of oral history and the available records. It examines the background to the mobilization of the Battalion in December 1941; who they were and for what they were trained, their equipment and the Battalion as a family with its own spirit. It relates the Battalion's series of disasters at Moulmein, Sittang and Bilin involving the crossings of the Salween, Sittang and Bilin rivers, Hmawbwi, Toksan and Yenangyaung – which left them increasingly less able to fight as a unit, with diminishing numbers and equipment – and finally, the exhausting march from Monywa to the crossing of the Chindwin River and over the last mountains to Tamu on the Indian border and relative safety. The book ends by detailing the factors that prevented optimum military performance and those other factors that made the cohesion of this Battalion from start to finish – and individual survival – possible.

This work is above all an appreciation of the extraordinary powers of recovery which the men of the Battalion, most of whom were not professional soldiers, showed again and again. The fact that the Battalion survived as a unit after so many days of the gruelling 1942 Burma campaign – surely the longest exposure of infantry to warfare in retreat in the history of the British Army – is simply remarkable. About a fifth of the men were killed and left with no known grave.

The details of the Battalion's involvement have already been published as the fifth volume of the history of the regiment (Kingston, 1950) from the recent memories of those who took part. This gave the necessary details of many individual acts of heroism and fortitude and no purpose would be served by repetition, but the citations of two of the three non-commissioned officers who received the Military Medal – Howson, Steerment and Butler – are given in Appendix B.

Ralph and David Tanner

An Overview

The British political and military position in Burma 1941

The position of the 2/KOYLI in Burma at the start of the war with Japan in December 1941 is defined by the German war centred on the defence of the United Kingdom. Burma was on the very fringe of British strategic concerns. This can be demonstrated by the fact that the Burma Army headquarters in Rangoon in 1941 'was very small and in fact no larger than a normal second class district headquarters in India. It had neither the know-how nor the staff capacities to effect the changes to put Burma onto a war footing' (Grant and Tamayama 1999: 39). There were just two British infantry battalions in Burma and a number of military police and Burma Rifle battalions, which had not been trained to confront a professionally trained and organised enemy.

On mobilisation, the 2/KOYLI became part of the 1st Burma Brigade in the 1st Burma Division, which had been created with two other Brigades using the eight Burma Rifle battalions together with the 13th Indian Infantry Brigade of three regular Indian infantry battalions, which arrived in March 1941. This meagre force was added to before Rangoon fell by the creation of the 17th Division with the arrival of the experienced 7th Armoured Brigade (less one regiment) from the Middle East – with Stuart tanks better armed than any Japanese tanks – and the 63rd Infantry brigade with three further Indian infantry battalions. Following a visit to 17th Division at Kyaiktko on February 6, General Wavell had noted on a train journey from Pegu to the Sittang that the flat, open topography was good tank country. The 7th Armoured was duly despatched, '... for which everyone who served in Burma in 1942 had cause to be grateful to Wavell' (James Lunt, *A Hell of a Licking* 1986). Additionally, also in March, the Inniskilling Battalion was flown into Magwe in American aircraft. While this total looks impressive enough on paper, their experience of modern warfare – with the exception of the 7th Armoured Brigade – was limited to internal security and guerrilla warfare on the arid North-West Frontier of India.

In contrast, the Japanese Army used four divisions with appropriate support staff, with the majority of men having already experienced combat in China. The Japanese air force had at least 200 aircraft with additions from Malaya and the Philippines after the campaigns there finished, against which the Royal Air Force and the American Volunteer Group probably never have had more than fifty. With this inequality in numbers, equipment and professionalism, it may seem surprising that the campaign lasted so long, particularly as the Japanese planned to march off-road and used only light equipment while the British and Indian units were 'road-bound' in attitude and experience. In short, the Japanese army invaded Burma well equipped and trained for what they intended to do, but out-of-date in terms of Western (to that date, largely apolitical) planning and industrial might. The British and Indian units were about to learn their trade behind the mountain barriers along the Indian-Burma border which the Japanese had learnt several years earlier in China. The British-Indian army was unprepared for a war which they had hoped to avoid and which they could not afford to fight. The fact that so many survived and their subsequent success is a tribute to their quality and that of their supporting staff.

A military biography of Capt. R.E.S. Tanner. 223473

In order to ensure as much accuracy as possible in this history, Ralph Tanner asked for his personal details from the Army Records, expecting a page giving some dates and general information. Three months later he received some two hundred pages of documents relating to his military career from 4 September 1939 until leaving the regular army reserve of officers on 5 October 1971. It is a salutary reminder to those who write about their experiences half a century before that he could not remember many of the details recorded in these documents and had inaccurate memories of other parts. In such a comprehensive coverage largely dealing with his ill-health after the 1942 Burma campaign – on account of which he was repatriated in 1943 – it was strange that there was no note of his being Mentioned in Despatches in the *London Gazette* on 30 December 1941, in connection with the Layforce (Commando) operations in Crete following the German airborne invasion of the island. The formal citation was hung on his study wall.

On enlisting at the Artist Rifles depot in Dukes Road London on the Monday after war was declared, he was classed as an officer cadet as he had passed Certificate A at Rugby. Nothing, however, materialised from this enlistment. He then re-enlisted in North London on 25 May 1940 and was posted as a private to a battalion of the Queens Regiment in Aldershot. After an apparent mistaken posting to the Bedfordshire and Hertfordshire Regiment in Bedford, he ended up as part of a Special Tank Hunting platoon in the Brock barracks depot of the Royal Berkshire Regiment in Reading on 28 September 1940, where he was put through an anti-tank course.

On volunteering for No. 3 Commando he was posted to Largs on 25 October 1940 and went through a Combined Operations course and later volunteered for foreign service with 8 Commando, leaving Britain on 31 December on HMS *Glenroy*. As batman to Evelyn Waugh – the novelist, then a Royal Marine captain acting as the Intelligence officer for the Commando Brigade – he took part in the Commando raid on Bardia on 15 March 1941. His military records show that he embarked on HMS *Isis* for Crete at Alexandria on 15 May 1941, which appears to be incorrect, as No. 8 Commando were sent to Crete after the German invasion had started on 20 May. He left Crete on HMS *Abdiel* on 1 June, the last Allied ship to leave the island. His Mention in Despatches was awarded for his action in delivering a message from Colonel Laycock, Commander Layforce, to the rearguard on the night of 31 May/1 June. As a result of the loss of so many men as POWs, the Middle East Commandos were disbanded and rather than going into a pool of infantry replacements for the Western Desert on 15 October 1941, Ralph Tanner volunteered to join a small party going to Burma. This party became part of Military Mission 204 destined for China, and were trained in demolitions at Maymyo, a north-eastern Burma hill station known as the Bush Warfare School.

The selective nature of memory – particularly in extreme and stressful situations – is exemplified by the fact that Ralph Tanner has no recollection of the moment or the process of his battlefield commission from a Private to a 2/Lieut. According to a cipher telegram to London he was commissioned as a 2/Lieut into the 2/KOYLI on 1 January 1942, a rather abrupt transition from private without having gone through any officer training course, after a single interview. He recalls his first duty as an officer as having to mount the depot guard. He then joined the Battalion's headquarters for the second part of the Burma campaign and the retreat, falling sick with dysentery at Tamu just before the Battalion left Burma for good.

Then followed a long period in the tented 17th British General Hospital in Dehra Doon, after which he was posted to take an Intelligence course at Karachi and stayed on as an Instructor in Japanese tactics at the Far Eastern School of Intelligence. This was followed by further ill-health so he was repatriated to Britain. Having been graded as unfit for foreign service he was sent on a general Intelligence course at the Intelligence Corps depot at Rotherham, and another one on Japanese Intelligence at Matlock. On 10 January 1944 he was posted to the War Office in Whitehall as an Intelligence Officer in section MI2d dealing with the Japanese Army, its equipment and order of battle, working with captured documents and wireless intercepts. He volunteered for Civil Affairs in Burma on 4 May 1945 for which he went through a course in Wimbledon and went back to Burma via India on a draft which started from London on 24 July 1945. In Burma he was posted to Lashio in the Northern Shan States, from where he was demobilised in October 1946, having been taken on as a probationer in the Burma Frontier Service.

List of Maps

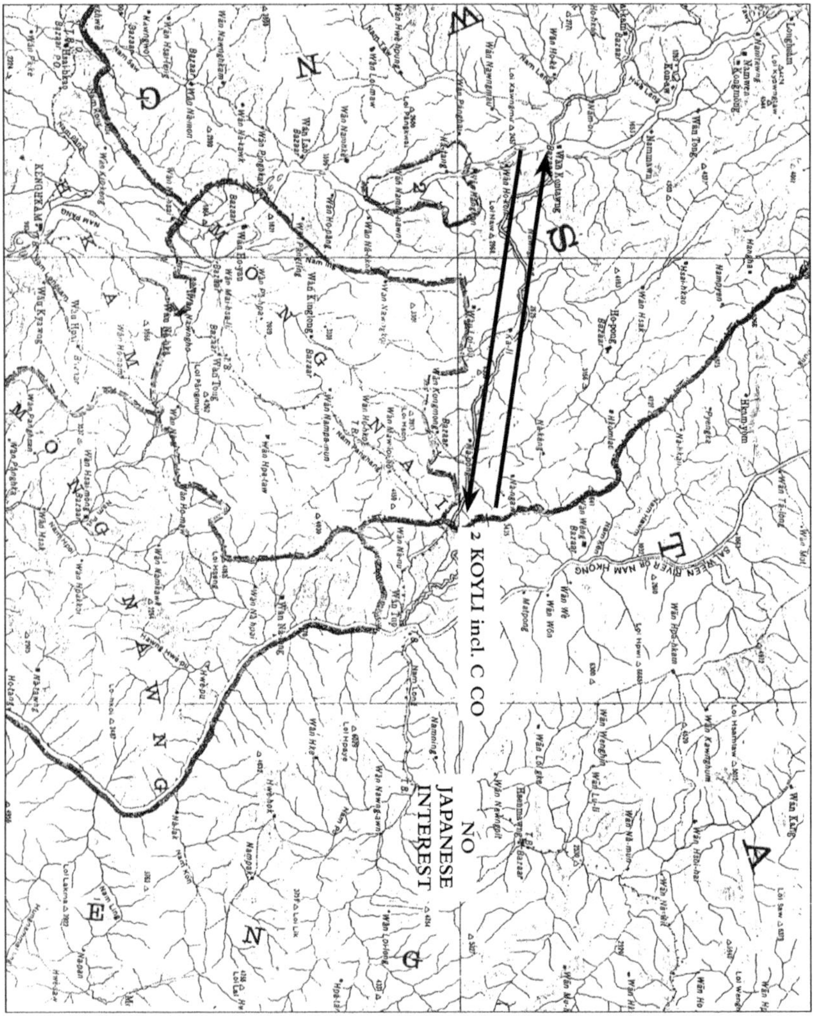

Map 1: Upper Burma, River Salween

The first 'river problem'. It had been assumed that the Japanese would invade Burma from Thailand in the east, so the Battalion made defensive positions at the River Salween. The Japanese never came this way and the Battalion suffered such heavy casualties from malaria that instead of evacuating west with the rest of the Battalion a forward hospital was constructed to cater for them.

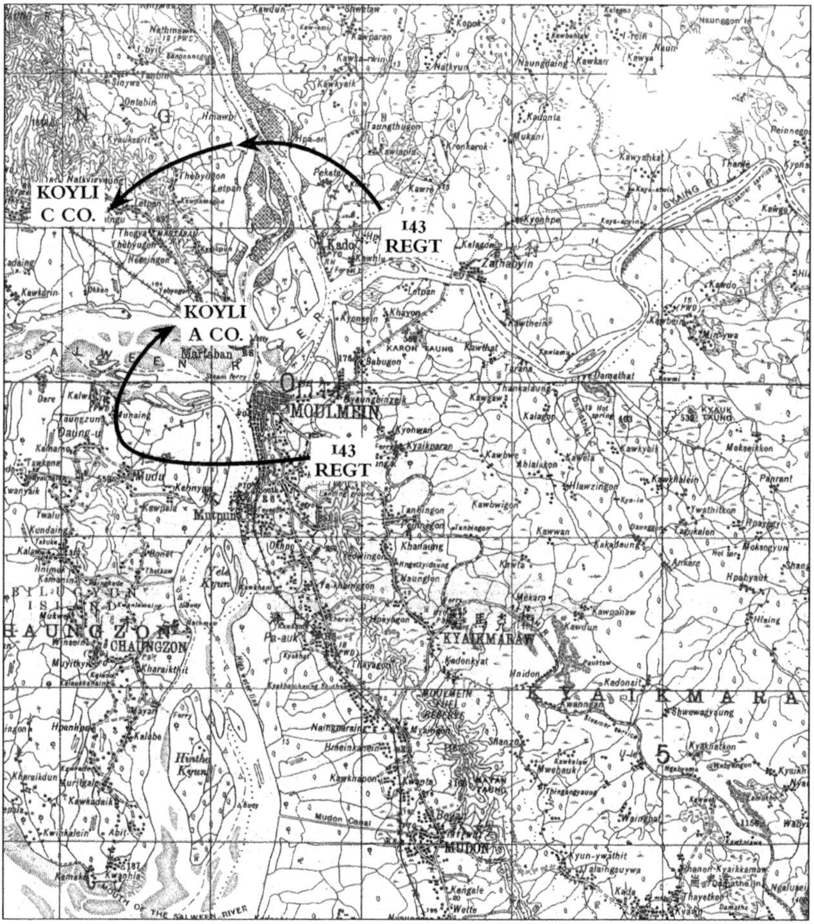

Map 2: Lower Burma, River Salween

The second river problem. Once it was apparent that the Japanese were coming over the mountains defensive positions were moved farther south, and the Regiment was given an enormous front to defend and was bypassed as a result.

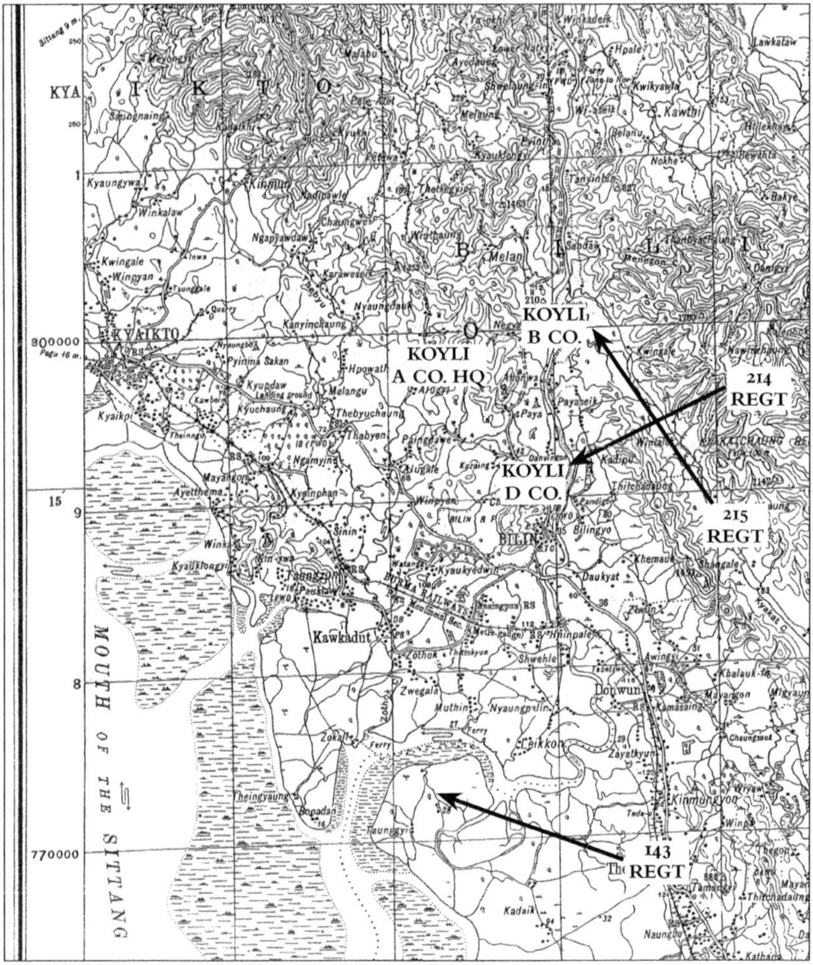

Map 3: Upper Burma, River Bilin

The third river problem. The Battalion was too spread out to do anything constructive and were bypassed again.

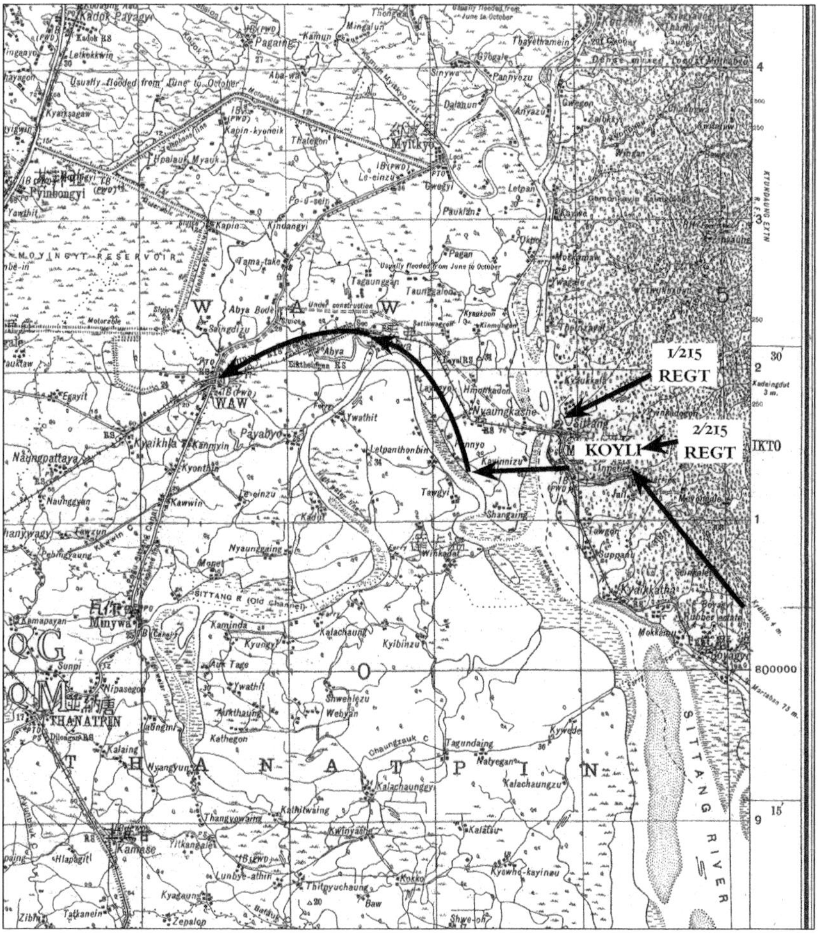

Map 4: Lower Burma, River Sittang
The fourth river problem. The scene of the much debated order to destroy the bridge on 23 February with two brigades on the wrong side, resulting in many men having to walk to Waw with no equipment and sometimes little clothing or footwear.

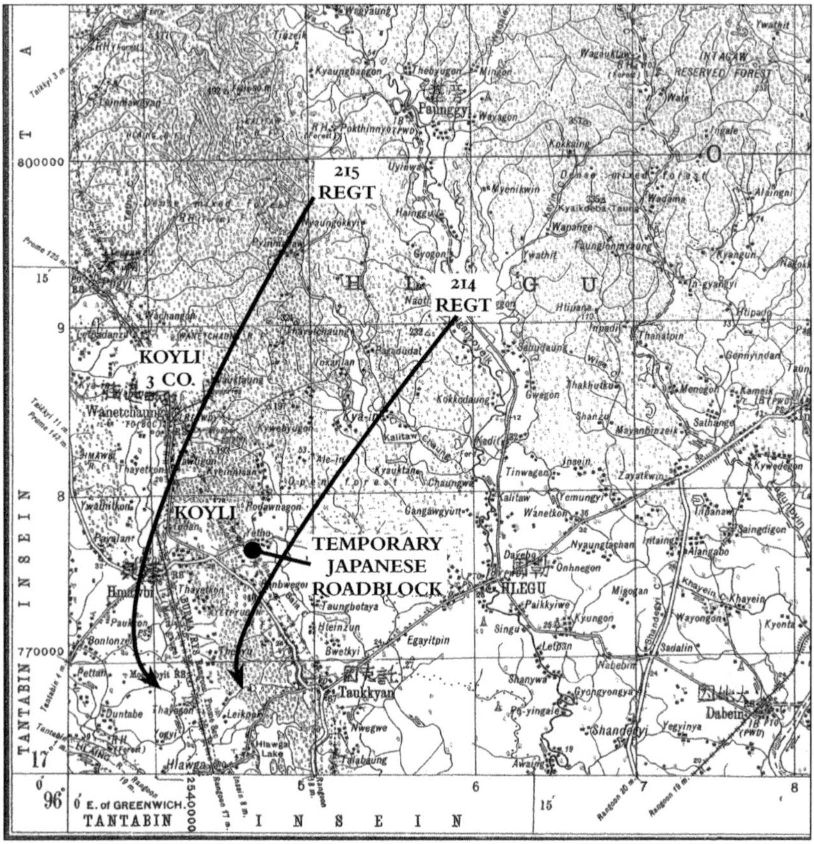

Map 5: Lower Burma, Taukkyan Road Block
The Japanese roadblock at Taukkyan was a potential disaster as it could have held up the British forces, instead the Japanese abandoned the position as they could not believe that Rangoon would not be defended.

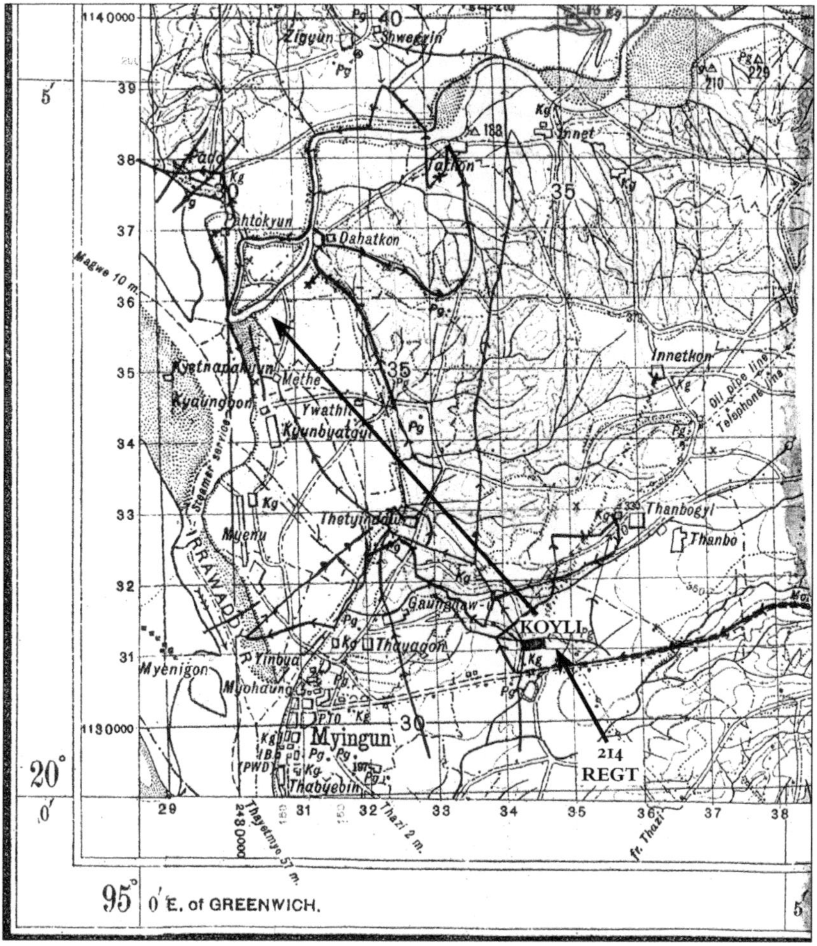

Map 6: Central Burma, Magwe area

This map gives an overview of the action on 14 April detailed in Map 10.

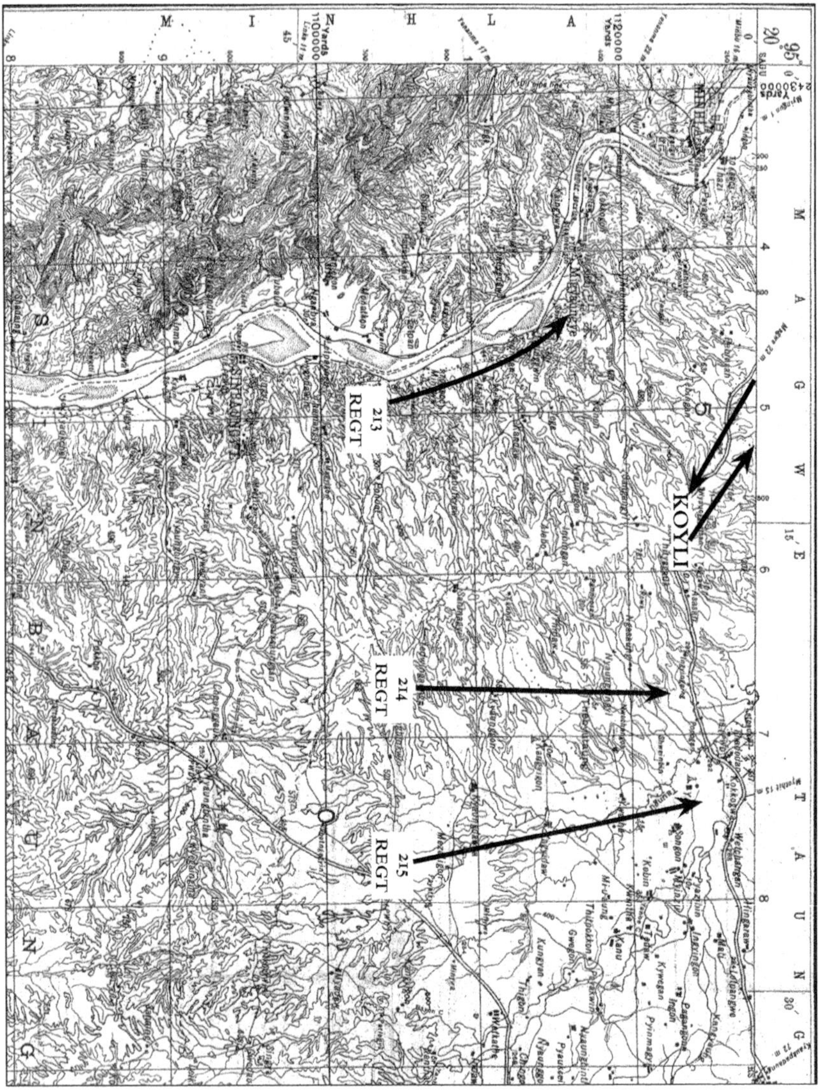

Map 7: Central Burma, Migyaungyee

Battalion listening posts reported Japanese movements in all areas, and as no orders were received, the Battalion abandoned their position at night. Minutes after they left the village in which they had been sheltering the Japanese attacked it.

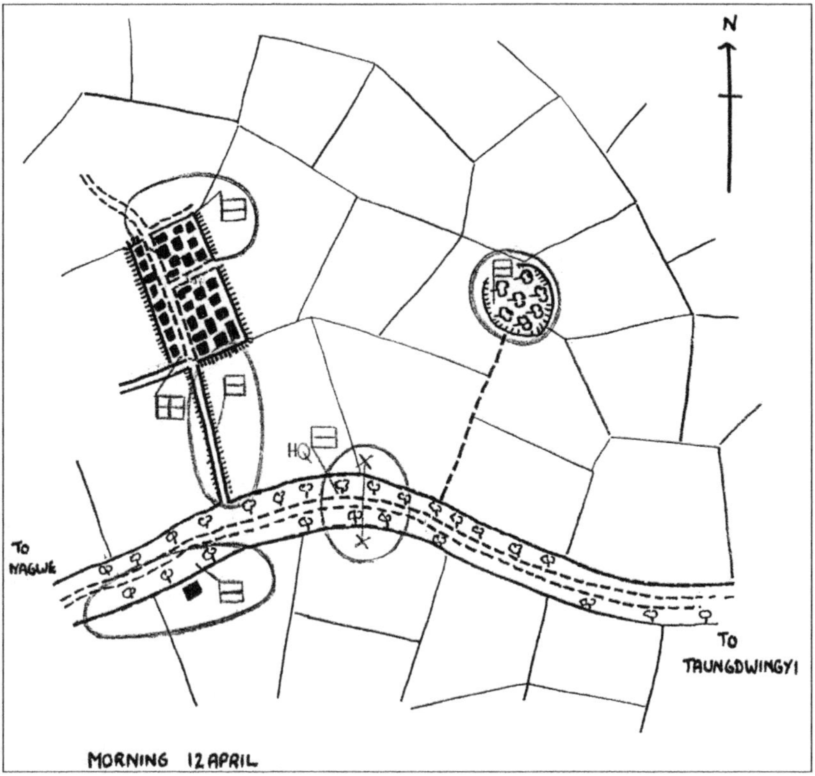

Map 8: Tanner sketch map, Magwe area, morning of 12 April
A roadblock was formed with a broken-down bullock cart and some wood and stones, and Lt Fitzpatrick sited his mortars behind some bushes to the north edge of the road. Ralph Tanner recalls being located in the village to the north-west of the sketch.

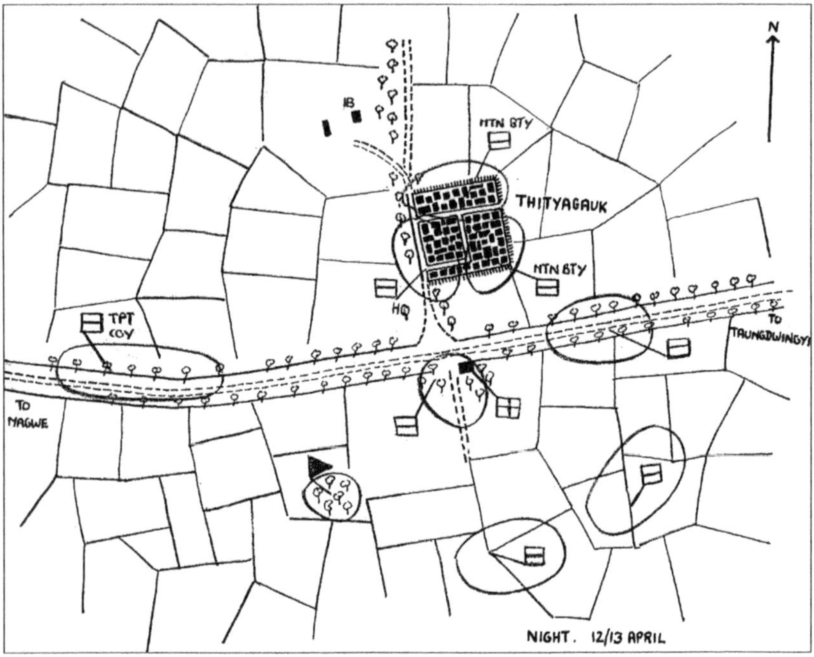

Map 9: Tanner sketch map, Magwe area, night of 12/13 April
Ralph Tanner's contemporary memory of the events, the dates on the sketch map and the diary differ. This is hardly surprising given the confusion of a mobile action at night, and the 67 years since the action. However, this is the only sketch showing a Mountain Battery but the diary mentions his boots being stitched by the Saddler from the Mountain Battery on 16 April.

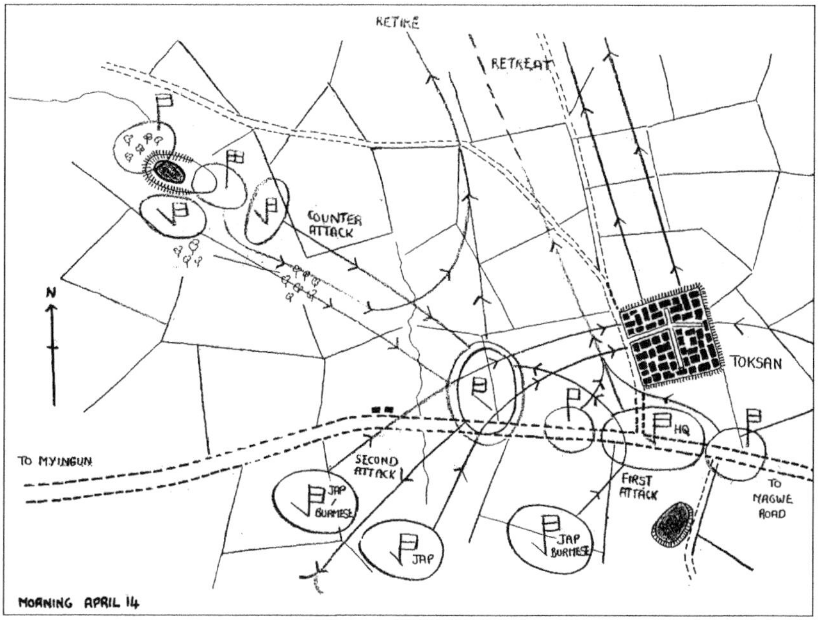

Map 10: Tanner sketch map, Magwe area, morning of 14 April
Ralph Tanner became accidentally adrift between the two forces and missed the action as he was out on patrol in the west central area of the sketch.

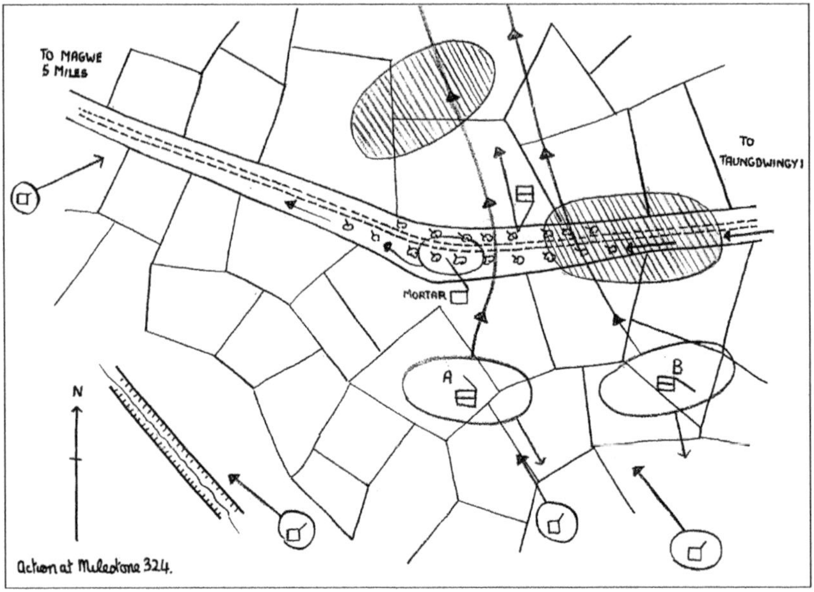

Map 11: Tanner sketch map, Magwe area action at milestone 324
2 KOYLI were carried by lorries from Magwe to block the road at milestone 324, which is not mentioned in the diary, but Ralph Tanner recalls being shelled and having to march northwards after the action in very hot and dusty conditions.

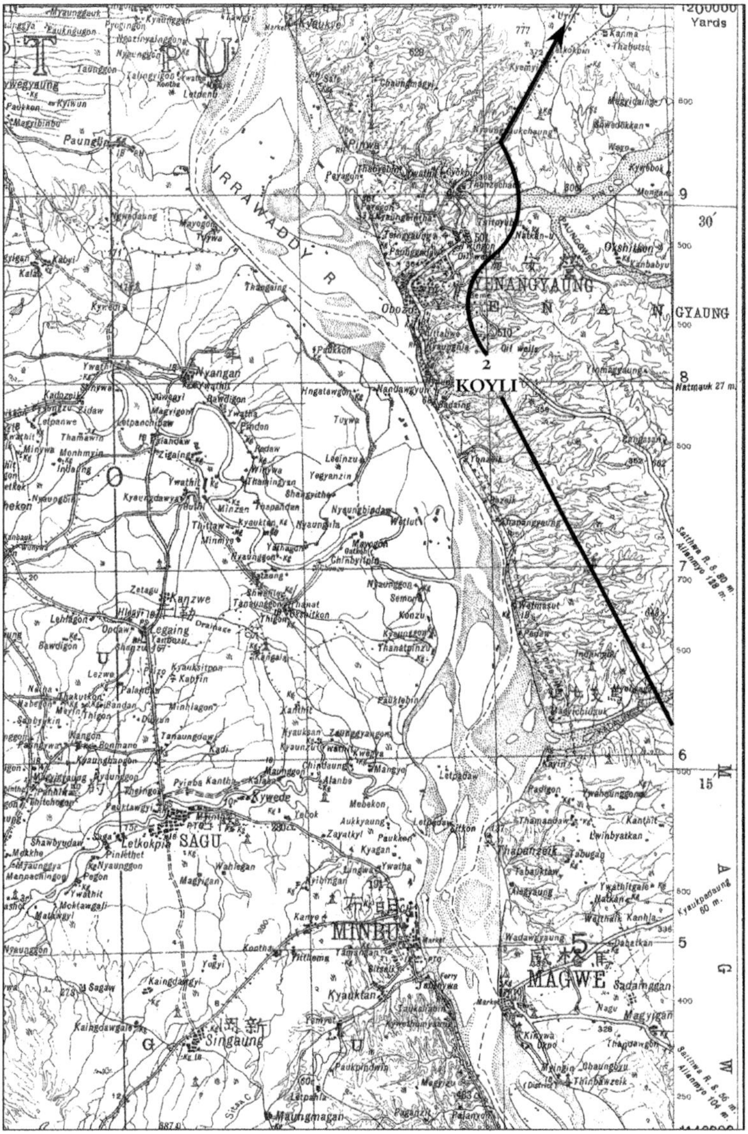

Map 12: Central Burma, Yenangyaung area

This is a macro view of the route taken by 2 KOYLI through Yenangyaung northwards.

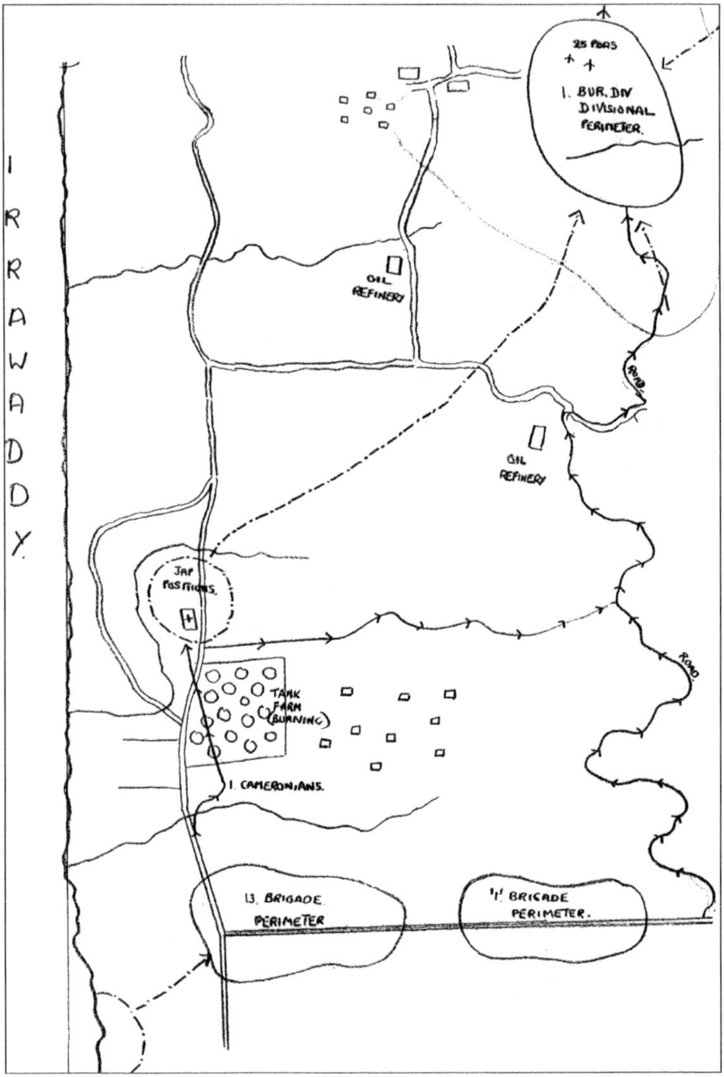

Map 13: Tanner sketch map, Yenangyaung action

This is perhaps a classic case of situational ambiguity or 'the fog of war' (attributed to Carl von Clausewitz, *On War*), which Ralph Tanner referred to as 'a shambles'. A very mobile action over a number of days made worse by the smoke and heat from a burning oilfield.

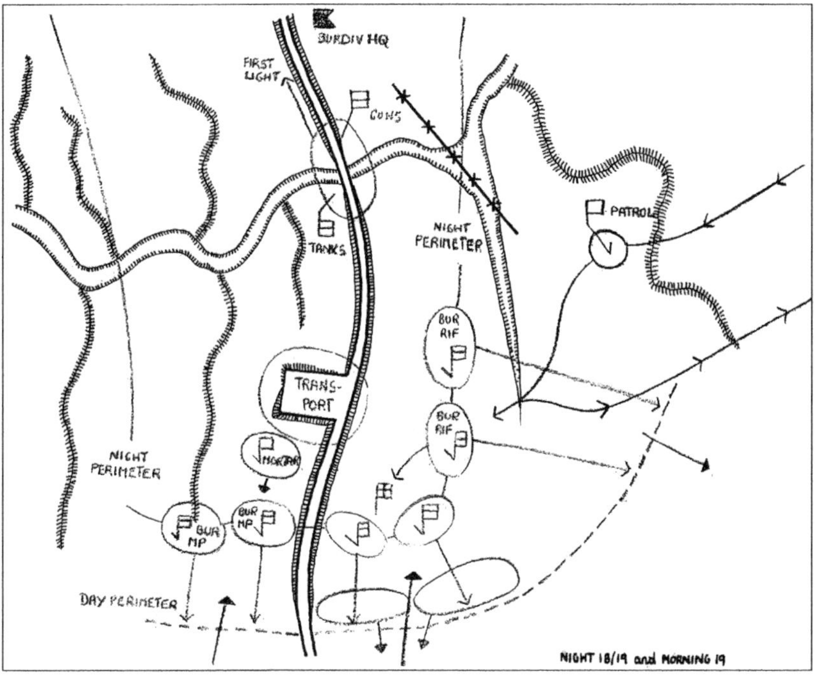

Map 14: Tanner sketch map, Yenangyaung action

Ralph Tanner's lasting memory of the action is being caught in a panic at night with his boots off; his own having come unstitched again and the pair 'borrowed' from a dead Indian soldier being too small. He also vividly recalls the gunners stripped to the waist manning the 25-pounders covering their withdrawal to the north.

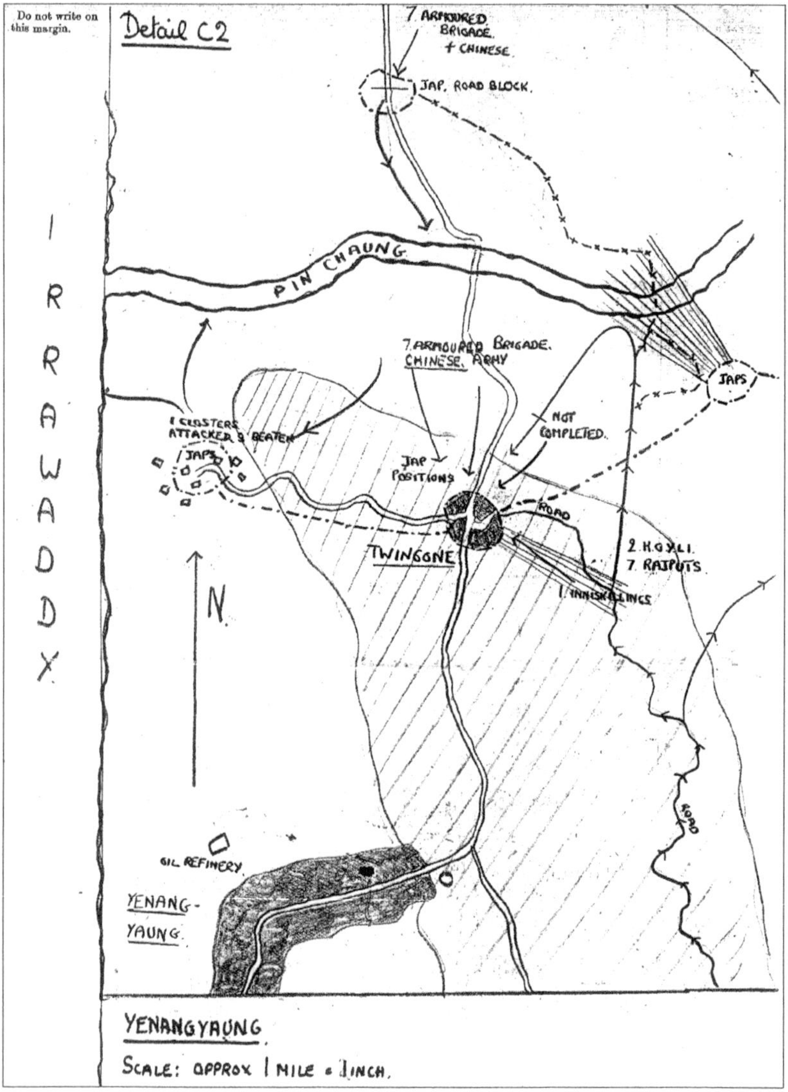

Map 15: Tanner sketch map, Yenangyaung action
After the Japanese roadblock to the north of the Pin Chaung, 2 KOYLI were able to retreat and cross the Pin chaung and access their first water for two days. See illustration 13.

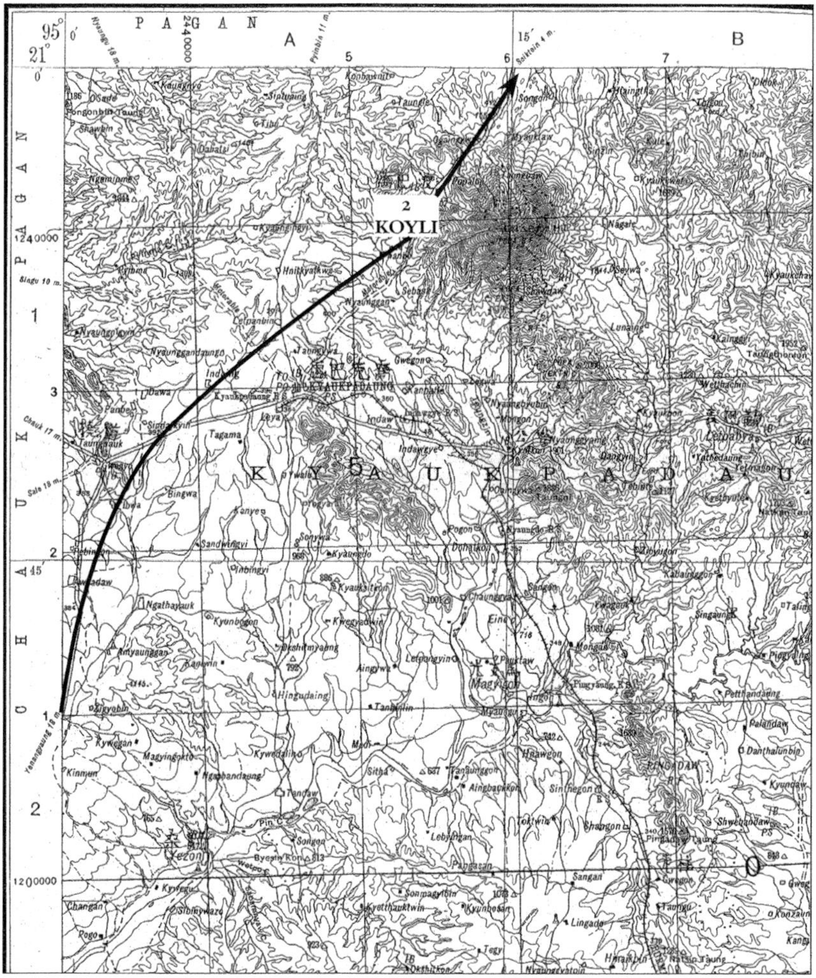

Map 16: Central Burma, Mount Popa area
After the action at Yenangyaung the Battalion were transported to Mount Popa.

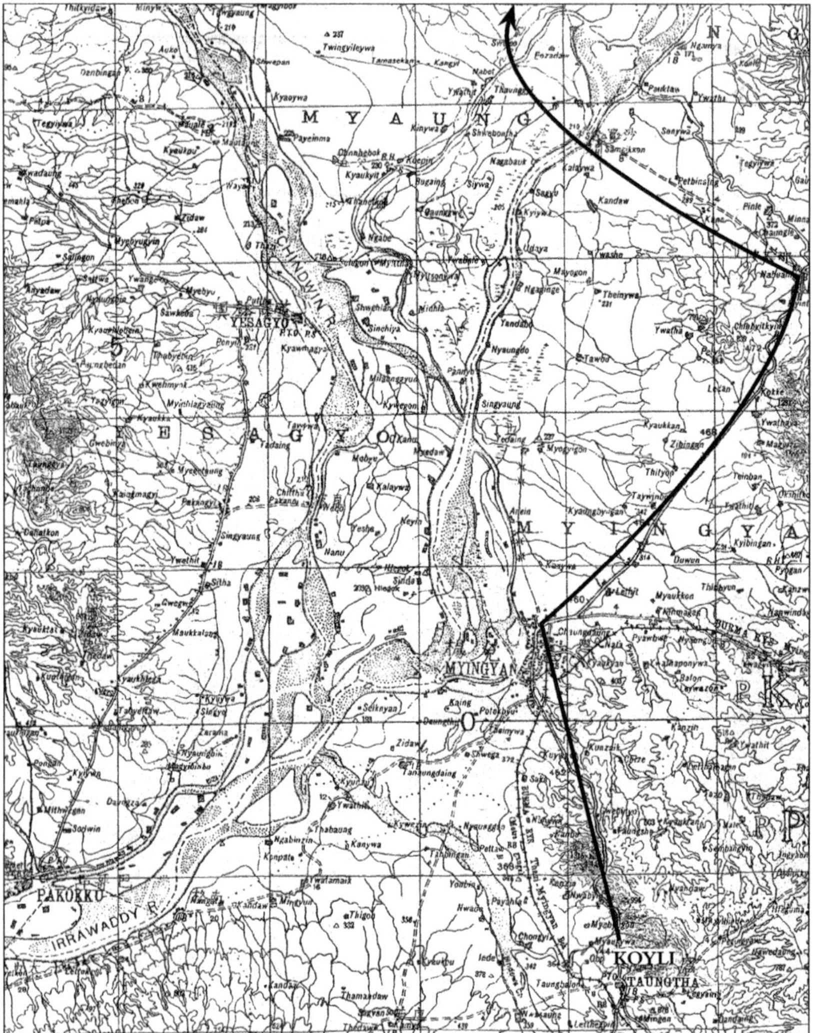

Map 17: Central Burma, Myingyan area
The Battalion marched all day and in the early night they marched through the completely deserted town of Myingyan. The Irrawaddy was crossed at Sameikkon with help from the Royal Marines.

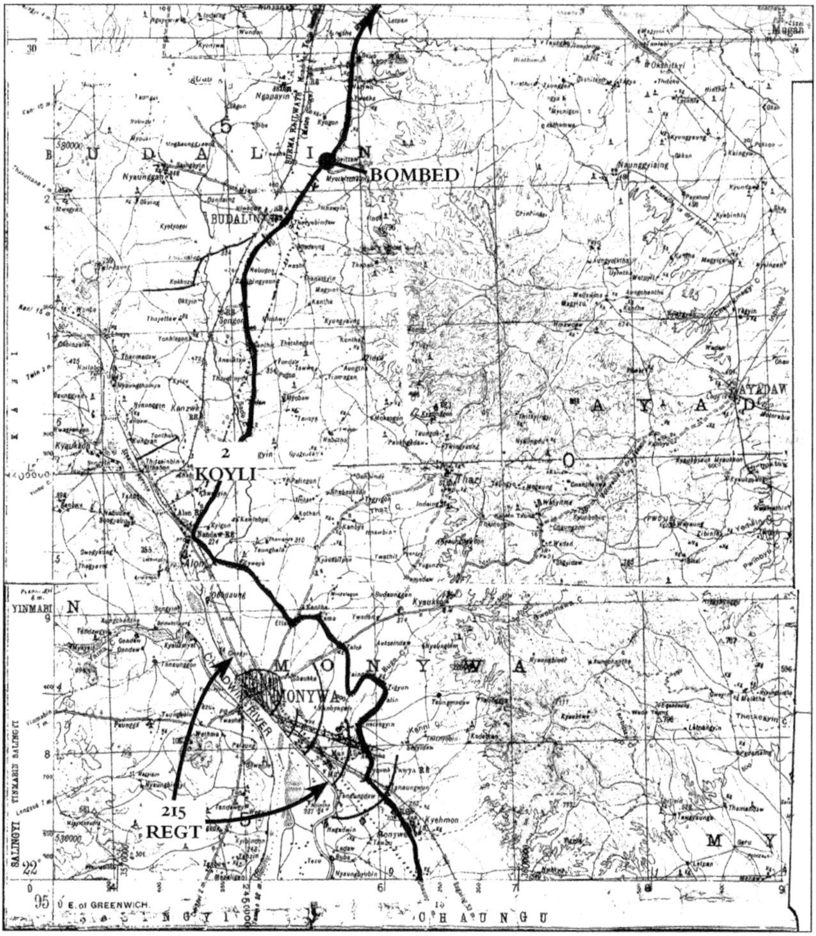

Map 18: Central Burma, Monywa area

The Battalion was supposed to go to Monywa by boat but the Japanese got there first so they marched out by night.

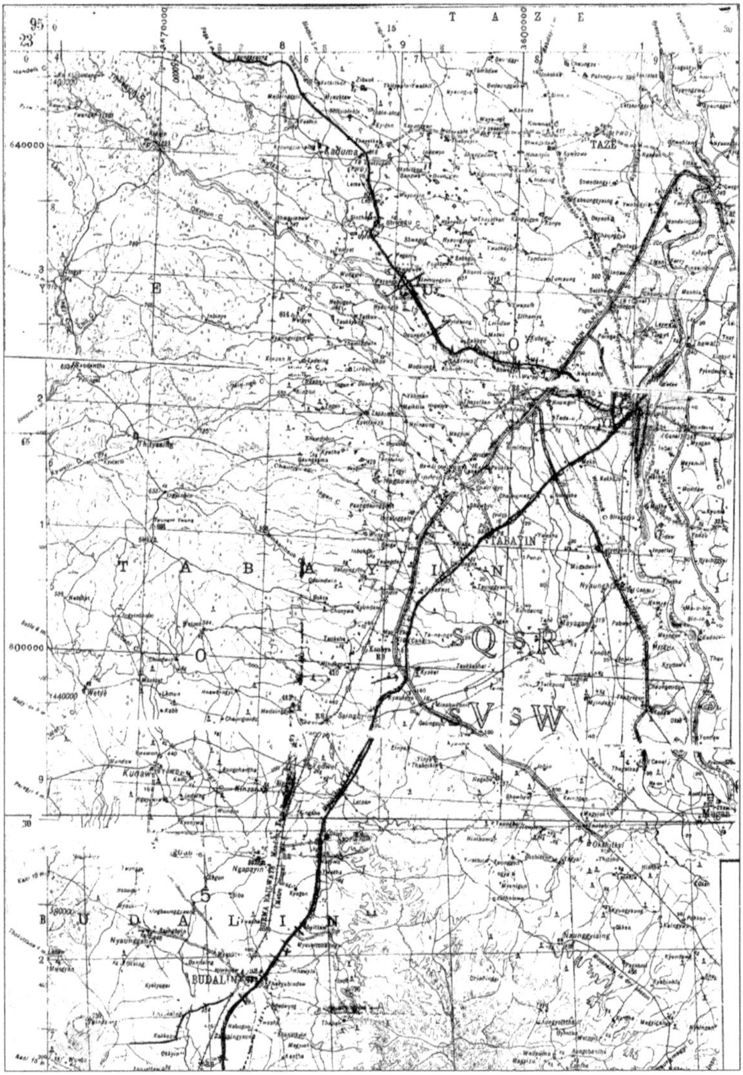

Map 19: The cut across country to India

Yeu, the town on the right hand side of the map was where Ralph Tanner and the Battalion were told to help themselves to food from a stockpile by the side of the road.

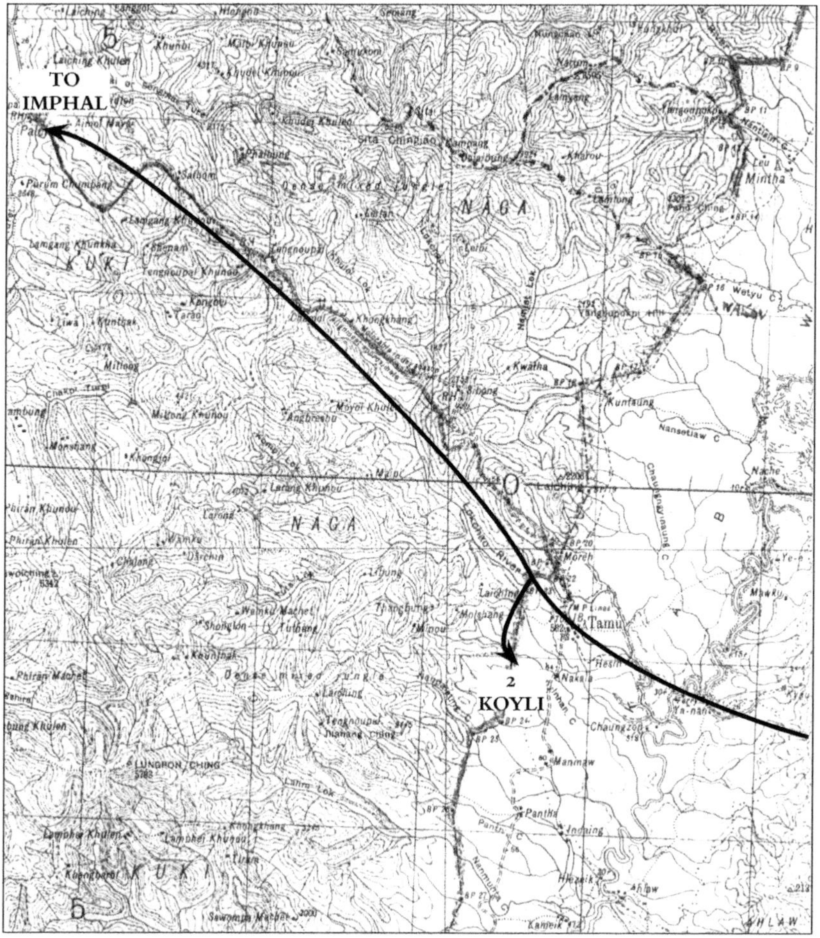

Map 20: The cut across country to India
Ralph Tanner was taken sick with dysentery at Tamu and transported by lorry to Palel and Imphal in India. The remainder of 2 KOYLI marched 3–4 miles south to defend the road to Kalewa.

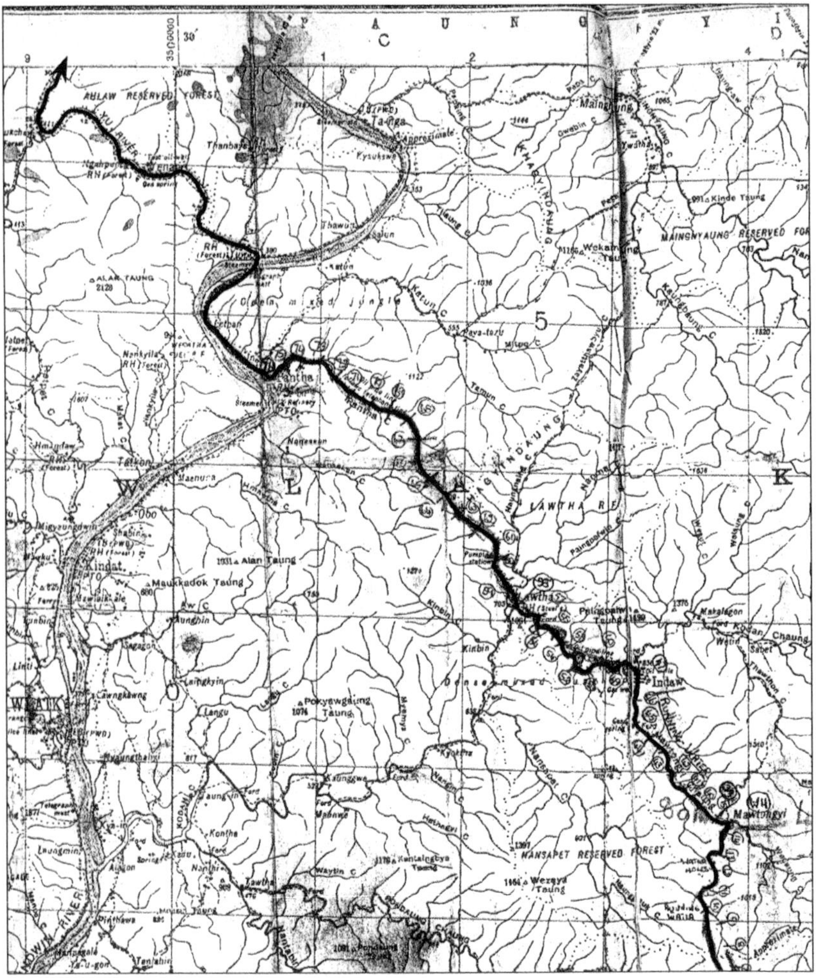

Map 21: Marching stages as marked by Tanner

The fifth river problem. This is a copy of the map carried by Ralph Tanner on which he marked the hourly stopping places. The River Chindwin crossing at Yuwa on 14 May is just north of Kantha in the north west corner of the map.

Chapter 1

The Past is a Foreign Country[1]

What the Second Battalion of the King's Own Yorkshire Light Infantry did in the first five months of the Japanese invasion of Burma was extraordinary by any standards of military performance. The men showed bravery and an impressive ability to adapt to diminishing resources; the survivors marched over a thousand miles to get back to India. It is too easy in the historical studies of warfare to concentrate on political failings and the inadequacies of senior officers, because at those levels there are always quantities of documents on public record which can be analysed and which of course leave out the personal realities of warfare. Similarly, the failure of military units to perform optimally is often assessed by well-intentioned scholars who were not there and may have had little personal experience of prolonged danger and physical deprivation; they will never have gone without water, been blown sideways by bombs, had sores on their feet from marching and watched Japanese soldiers coming near to their hiding place. Only the highly imaginative novelist can begin to express what these men experienced.

Too much of the writing about the initial shocks of Japanese aggression has involved the laying of blame and playing the 'if' game, suggesting that performance and outcomes could have been different. This Battalion of infantry was certainly dealt a poor hand, but it is no part of this study to discuss why this was so, except to say that defence against German attack would always have priority over Burma, which only became a war front long after most of the pieces on the strategic chess board had already been committed. This study attempts to show how these soldiers played the cards which they were given and in the words of one officer who survived, how they 'got on with it'. This was achieved through a combination of personality, trained performance, regimental and personal backgrounds, the equipment they had and the circumstances with which they were faced, over which they had almost no control at all.

The availability of war records

We know the results of the battles of Waterloo, Kursk and El Alamein but what it meant to the hundreds of thousands of men who were present and the small combat units in which they spent their days of war is less known.

The availability of records to historians after a campaign is over takes three forms; but paper on which records are kept will not survive unless someone or some institution has an interest it preserving it. A private soldier who served in the British army for up to the five years of World War II would have left an enormous paper trail involving his pay, promotions, training courses and movements. Ralph Tanner estimated that between June 1940 and sometime in 1946 when he was demobilised in Burma, his name must have been on at least a thousand documents, and yet at the end of this period he found just six official pieces of paper that can establish that he had any military existence at all.

In more or less static warfare in which base areas are not overrun by the enemy, there is always a flow of paper from front units to the rear areas from both sets of combatants so there are both public and private records available, should those involved retain them. Enormous quantities are available from Flanders in World War I and the Middle East and India in World War II. Then there is the paper trail left behind by successful advancing armies, but this is much less in quantity, so that it has to be augmented by historians talking to those involved, as in the 1944 siege of Kohima (Colvin 1994, Edwards 2009) and for the subsequent advance into Burma (Cooper 1973, Fraser 1999), which are virtually written oral histories relying on memory and records still in existence.

Finally there are military retreats such as Burma in 1942 in which the only paper records are a limited number of top-level wireless messages sent back to India. Similarly, the Imperial War Museum and the National Army Museum hold very little data about the battle for Crete in May 1941 at which Ralph Tanner was present and indeed in correspondence with an Australian historian wanting to find out details of the final evacuation from Khora Sphakion and was quoted in a study of that battle (Beevor 1991). There is even less data available about Burma in 1942 relating to the Second Battalion of the King's Own Yorkshire Light Infantry. There is very little evidence on paper of the experiences of these 500 men and only their well-intentioned memories which made up subsequent reports, diaries and indeed the official War Diary for the Battalion written by Lt. Col. Chadwick, who commanded for the last half of the campaign, though he was absent for some part of the earlier months through illness.[2] In the early days, letters may have been written but none are available in any known records. Censorship would have ensured that they contained little information anyway. Ralph Tanner may have received some letters but his parents received nothing from him for at least three months, and ones addressed to him circulated round a number of possible Indian addresses.

The official history of this Second Battalion in the Burma campaign (Hingston 1950) was not written by a participant and there are no references in it as to the sources from which so much detail about individual behaviour and events was obtained. Yet it mentions over one hundred men in particular events. Presumably it was created from the War Diary and other reports and personal contacts with survivors, but very little is now available in the Light Infantry depot at Pontefract, the original home of the regiment before it was abolished as a locally recruited unit by merging into a single Light Infantry Regiment. This thorough work did not use Ralph Tanner's diary, because its existence was not known to the regiment.

There is a printed casualty list for all battalions of the regiment which lists dates of presumed deaths in Burma with their dates of recruitment, but there appears to be only Ralph Tanner's hand-written diary from March to May 1942 available as a primary source. Included in this book are the relevant parts of the original maps of ground covered by the battalion with, in some cases, his marking in pencil of the location of the hourly halts, the photographs which Ralph Tanner took, and some sketch maps of the various actions at which he was present. The only other primary document retained by the Battalion are hand-written details in an official alphabetical Register of Deserters, with 'deserters' replaced by the word 'missing', of all non-commissioned members of the Battalion. In some cases against 'missing' is the word 'located' in another hand.

Then there is John Heald's hand-written roll listing some 600 names of officers and men with their army numbers giving dates for individuals missing, wounded, and killed and in some cases nicknames, short anecdotes and comments (Appendix D). This monumental hand-written work shows great personal devotion to the Battalion of which he was a member in India after this campaign. The roll was completed in 1985 relying upon the memories of men involved forty years after the events listed. He must have had some help from regimental records that existed then so as to be able to include so many army numbers. We do not know how much he got right as he lists Ralph as a captain and the transport officer for the battalion, which he was not. There is also his history of the campaign which did use his diary, so it seems likely that both these works were created after the regimental history had been written. The Fitzpatrick book of his personal memories (Fitzpatrick 2001) is an even later production and may not be classifiable as a primary source, paralleling Fraser's account of the Border Regiment's platoon (Fraser 1992).

The Second Battalion of the King's Own Yorkshire Light Infantry took part in the Burma campaign of early 1942 from start to finish but neither the nominal roll for the Battalion in 1941, nor the survivor roll of those who arrived in India has survived. Thus more than five hundred men have passed into history in the service of their country with very little evidence that they were even there. What records do exist as evidence of the presence of these men as individuals rather than just as part of a corporate mass are the telegrams of the higher command to their superiors; including a telegram of congratulations from the Queen as Colonel-in-Chief of the regiment about their performance at Toksan – which they never received.

If we take the comparable situation of an infantry battalion in the Western Desert, Italy, and then in Western Europe, the amount of documents subsequently available to historians is huge. There would have been daily war diary entries kept up-to-date and sent to higher formations, casualty lists as well as Part One and Part Two orders, as well as letters home and personal data recorded in each soldier's AB64, which he kept in his personal possession. In London after D-Day some thirty censor officers each read about three hundred letters every day for a month and a proportion of these letters would have been kept by the recipients as personal treasures, particularly if these men became casualties.

The records held by the Light Infantry Office for the King's Own Yorkshire Light Infantry – which no longer exists – contain no data at all which originated in Burma. There is the post facto War Diary, which under the circumstances of 'regular' warfare would have been written up regularly, but that was not the case with this Battalion. This War Diary is a compilation from memory of the then battalion commander Major Chadwick, with the help of other survivors who had returned or who had remained with the Battalion at Shillong in September 1942, and data from the records of I Bur Brigade and I Bur Div, which reached India by signal. The documentation available from these higher formations is perforce scant on detail regarding the Battalion.

At Pontefract there is a file containing substantial correspondence about getting compensation for the regimental silver which was buried near to Pyingaing and which was stolen during the occupation and never recovered, but there is no nominal roll of members of the Battalion available either before they were mobilised or later. There is only a final casualty list of deaths in all battalions in all theatres of war between 1939–45, including, for example, accidental deaths in a blizzard in Iceland and those who died in accidents or in hospital in the United Kingdom. This list gives the names of those killed in action, died of wounds or missing presumed dead in action or as prisoners of war, with the date of their enlistment and the date of their presumed deaths. Of those who died in Burma in action, all 122 have no known grave; nor do those who died as prisoners of war, as, in time, the wooden crosses marking graves were used as firewood for the cooking fires of the surviving POWs. There is correspondence with the reformed Battalion at Shillong in Assam, endeavouring to find out what had happened to those who were listed as missing, but the surviving letters just list names, regimental numbers and dates when they were presumed missing and the dates when they were reported as missing on Army Form AFW3014, dated May and July 1942, signed by the Colonel Commanding and addressed to the Commandant No 6 Infantry Training Depot, Berwick-on-Tweed, with copy to Commandant KOYLI

Depot Party, Queen Elizabeth Barracks, Strensall. The listing of a name cannot be taken as conclusive evidence of the death of a missing man since we know of one case in which a soldier so listed married to a Burmese woman was hidden by her throughout the Japanese occupation in a village near to Mandalay.[3] There is a handwritten alphabetical register in an official foolscap notebook listing the names of those involved with 'missing' written against a number of names and the date on which they were last seen. Against 35 names it is noted that they were subsequently located in India. Who wrote this, where and when is not known, and the notations of 'located' against some names are in a different handwriting. What documentation, then, is available which could be considered as hard evidence? Very little and from only one source. Ralph Tanner took some 35 mm photographs dated after Yenangyaung of officers who can be named and of the column on the move or halted north of Pyingaing, and there is his tattered map, marking with pencil lines the hourly halts. It appears that this is the sum total of evidence of the Battalion's activities independent of a person's interpretation of events from memory.

When the hand-written diary written up within a year of the campaign's end is compared with the Battalion's official history written by Lt. Col. Hingston, it is obvious – assuming that Ralph was trying to write down the truth – that he never knew about or did not remember many events that happened more or less before his eyes. A ten-page report dated 1944 on the Battalion's activities from Yenangyaung onwards, written by Major Throckmorton and added to by Captain Anne, both of whom participated in the retreat, is in error in at least one instance: a patrol that Ralph Tanner recalled leading is recorded as being led by another officer with two men, of whom only one survived, wounded. Ralph Tanner led this patrol with two men, both of whom survived unwounded.[4] The detailed regimental history with drawings and diagrams which was published in 1950 lists by name the activities of no less than 166 officers and men and the extraordinary acts of some and the deaths of others, compiled from the memories of those involved, but when these records were made is not known. But it certainly made a vivid story and nobody seems to have objected to what had been written, or wished to add information.

Then there are the Japanese regimental records. Ralph Tanner visited Tokyo in 1985 and was entertained to lunch by surviving officers of 214 and 215 Infantry Regiments (Photo 1), equivalent to the British and Indian brigades of the 33 Division. They gave him a history of the Division's involvements, which included the Yenangyaung action (Appendix C and C/1).[5] This had been published in the 1970s and was nowhere near as extensive as the usual Japanese regimental histories, which are sometimes over 1,300 pages long. The Japanese have also produced a number of individual unit histories and compilations of the memories of soldiers who fought in Burma on the basis of the prefectures from which they were recruited.[6]

In between the dates of the British and Japanese printing of regimental and divisional records there is the monumental work of J. Heald, as discussed earlier, who joined the Battalion in India after the Burma campaign and started then and subsequently in Britain to work on its history; an extraordinary act of personal devotion to the Regiment to which he belonged as a wartime conscript. He wrote his own history of the campaign from his personal contacts; but more importantly he produced a roll of every soldier's name that he could find who was in Burma, with their regimental number when located.

Finally, there is the history of the Japanese 1942 invasion of Burma written by British and Japanese historians. Kazuo Tamayama's account (Lunt 1986) who met Ralph Tanner when he was in Tokyo, includes a number of references to the Battalion and comments favourably on their fighting qualities (Grant and Tamayama 1999). General Iida commanding the 15th Army writes in his post war memoir:

'Around Bilin we received strong and firm resistance by troops from British mainland, King's Own Yorkshire, who fought fiercely' (Iida 1990).

As to fictionalised accounts, one novelist, (Baxter 1955) served in the Battalion as an infantry officer and the other (Clifford 1960) was an officer in the Burma Rifles; they both give vivid impressions of what it must have been like to have been soldiers in those dark days, and the former in particular gives a moving account of relationships amongst men under conditions of continual stress.

The workings of memory

Individuals are likely to remember isolated and unusual events, the first occasion of seeing a dead man, hearing a bomb fall or bullets going overhead, but as these occasions repeated themselves there is less reason to remember their singularity and the possibility of inaccuracy must increase. Then, some time later, from a minute or two to half a century or more, as the result of some stimulus, a question from an outsider, a smell or something written or heard such as a whirring sound like a mortar shell descending, and some of these images are reactivated. Of course if a soldier from a patrol reports to his senior that he has seen something, it is generally assumed to be true unless there are reasons for disbelief due to that man's reputation, his nervousness, or the improbability of the report. But it seems likely that reports of Japanese numbers may well have been consistently exaggerated, since no one is likely to have counted what he saw or underplayed a threat.

It has been found (Clifford and Scott 1978) that an inaccurate recall of events is more likely when they are violent – attributable to the greater stress involved – and that evidence about a highly emotional incident should be treated with greater caution than that about a less emotional incident

(Loftus 1996). An interesting example of the memory failures of soldiers has been found at Gettysburg (Baddeley 1972). During the battle over 200 muzzle loading guns were found to have been loaded five or more times without being fired; one had been loaded 21 times without being fired once, yet those soldiers would have considered themselves to have been combatants and would have remembered themselves as such. In hindsight perhaps this could have been seen as a case of not wanting to fire (at a fellow American) and not wanting to be seen not to be firing. But this still works as a salutory reminder that memory is not a machine.

Ralph Tanner's account of the confused fighting in and around Toksan is interesting. The post-campaign War Diary covers this in detail, but does not mention the patrol on which Ralph was sent out and which resulted in his telling the Colonel that they had been bypassed by the Japanese. His diary makes no mention of this fighting and the activities of others during these two days but is very detailed as to his own experiences. Both documents were written months later and without any knowledge of what the other was writing. Much of what happened at Toksan was more or less under Ralph's nose but is largely absent from his written memories and most of what there is appears to be confused and different to the regimental history. As far as he can remember there was nothing in his own behaviour then which would have led his diary to be self-censored.

His record of what he experienced at Toksan and other eye-witness accounts may have been unconsciously adjusted to match the end of the story. Ralph Tanner lost his possessions there, so that he spent the remainder of the campaign with all that he owned in one small side haversack, and that applied to everyone else as well. It was to him very obviously a defeat; and so it remained in his memory until he met Japanese officers from 214 Regiment who had attacked them there, and their Regimental History – no doubt prepared with a better combination of paper records and memories than that of the British Battalion – showed that the British had killed 23 Japanese. In retrospect, this seemed a reasonable riposte in comparison to the British losses, so that his eye-witness judgement of a defeat became adjusted to a partial success. There seems little doubt that eye-witness testimony is not a particularly reliable source of information in assessing fighting.

Sometimes subsequent events may prove the inaccuracy of a personal memory. Ralph Tanner's diary records that he was the escorting officer taking the Battalion's wives and children from Maymyo and that the convoy started in the morning and spent the first night in the Burma Rifles barracks in Meiktila. Gerald Delaney, who as the 13-year-old son of the Regimental Sergeant Major was in the same convoy, later wrote that it left in the evening and spent the first night in Fort Dufferin, Mandalay. The Throckmorton/Anne record of Toksan refers to a patrol being sent out under 2/Lieut. Cranfield and two men who never returned, while Heald's roll gives the name of one man surviving and the patrol he led is not mentioned at all, although it was rescued by Lieut. Fitzpatrick who had seen them adrift through binoculars from where the Battalion was harboured.[7] This same account stated that the Battalion at Yenangyaung was lifted at nightfall by tanks, which took them across the Pin Chaung to the Divisional Collecting point, while Ralph's diary and a photograph which he took shows dispersed groups of men wading through the shallow water and indeed seeming to enjoy the available water after days of parched throats. An even better example of the fragility of long-term memories would be his own in relation to his diary written soon after getting out of Burma. He had not read this document since it was compiled in 1942/3. He found that he had little recollection of most of what he had described. Some commonplace events were remembered but some exceptional ones had completely gone. He described in detail an air raid on Magwe airfield which he watched from a rise well away from the area. He recalled numbers of aircraft attacking and that they did not machine-gun the buildings, as per the official record. It must have been like an air show but he only remembered going there later and photographing the wrecked aircraft, including P40s of the American volunteer Flying Tigers. He had no memories at all of the actual attack.

Perhaps the most poignant example of this memory failure is the story of another patrol in which he went out with three men. He knew the names of two of them from records and he advertised for them in the *British Legion* magazine in the 1990s and received no replies. Not surprisingly, for his own diary recorded that he went out with three men and came back with one, two were missing believed killed. Shakespeare makes the point in *Henry V*, in the famous speech before Agincourt: 'Old men forget; yet all shall be forgot, but he'll remember with advantages what feats he did that day.'

Ralph Tanner volunteered himself for a study of his memory by the Department of Experimental Psychology of the University of Oxford, based on his diaries, which the specialists involved had to believe he had not read since they were written. This involved him being subjected to some twenty tests of his intelligence and sixteen hours of being interviewed by three psychologists. They did not appear to find any major breakdown in remembering what had happened forty years previously – but principally because they had no personal knowledge of the everyday conditions under which the diary had been written – they were only able to look for logical inconsistencies. Ralph Tanner published a critique of the methodology used in 2001. We can see from this that what soldiers remember or do not remember is probably beyond contemporary research capabilities. We do not know the physical and much less the mental conditions of the soldiers in this Battalion in 1942, but we can assume that there was a progressive deterioration in what they were able to see and hear and remember afterwards; fear and food shortages would have ensured it. (See Appendix E.)

The nature of military truth is necessarily elastic and that we can only be certain of some key events. We know that the Sittang Bridge was blown on 23 February by Lieut. Ahmad Khan because it was a key event in the whole campaign and historians have concentrated on whether it was ordered to be blown too soon. However, for minor events we have only the reminiscences of survivors as to the circumstances in which Sergeant Majors Howson and Steerment earned their distinguished Military Medals (Appendix B). Is the tale of Private Bream apochryphal? He and a companion apparently missed his company moving off from Thaton station when the train to carry them back had not arrived, because they had gone to sleep in a quiet corner after having drunk a bottle or two of 'liberated' beer they had found. When the train did arrive, they woke up and found themselves alone, the train driver and fireman running off. They loaded the engine and tender with some supplies that had been abandoned and Bream drove the train back to catch up with the company, where he was received with acclamation; that is too good a story to have been invented. It was no doubt eminently memorable at a time when such accidental good news was more than welcome.

Leaving the dead (and the living) in peace

We know that 'the past is a foreign country' (L.P. Hartley 1953, Lowenthal 1997), so it behoves later writers on military events to be cautious in their assessments of what happened. While decision-making generals and politicians might be considered fair game for subsequent criticism, it is necessary to be humanely cautious. The events of distant history such as the Charge of the Light Brigade are beyond the personal concerns of anyone living. But World War II and perhaps even World War I are still matters of real concern to the living. The soldiers may no longer be alive, but their children will be. General Slim – commenting on the demeanour of survivors – wrote that they still acted as soldiers, despite their ragged appearance. From the point of view of someone who was there this could be called a kindly stretching of the truth, perhaps written with an eye to the families of men who did not make it (Slim 1956: 109–110). What such commanders wrote for confidential circulation within the military establishment was an altogether different matter and a necessary part of any army pulling itself together for future operations, as was the case in India in 1942 and 1943.

No one involved in warfare at whatever level will have been without some lapses of character and in conformity to duty which may have affected others, but most will be known only to individuals. It is an uneasy moral issue for erstwhile colleagues to disclose what they now in retrospect see as the failures of those with whom they fought and to whom they still have residual obligations as members of particular regiments. A recent book (Fitzpatrick 2001) contains statements about individuals which are at best unproven, statements about an officer being shot deliberately by his own men and the Regimental Sergeant Major being drunk. Harsh opinions based on memory have no part in military history unless they are supported by impartial documentation and by a range of memories.

Chapter 2

The Combatants

The Second Battalion of the King's Own Yorkshire Light Infantry was principally opposed by the Japanese 33rd Division composed of the 214 and 215 Regiments (comparable to the British-Indian Brigade), which had been formed as a division in 1939 and had already had combat experience in China. At the company level the Japanese may have had 200 men as opposed to the British-Indian 120 because their administrative 'tail' was much shorter; they expected their soldiers at all levels to get by with much less administrative and welfare support.

The divisional commander Seizo Sakurai and the regimental commanders Takanobu Sakuma and Munaji Harada were professionals, as were the British commanders, with the difference that the former had had considerable recent field experience of warfare, not just manoeuvres and actions in support of the civil power, a common activity of the Indian Army. Sakurai had passed out high from the Japanese Staff College and spoke French, having been their Military Attaché in France. He was a sophisticated and competent commander. These three senior Japanese officers had survived the weeding out of commanders who performed poorly – as occurs at the start of any war – and all were subsequently promoted.

The Battalion also met the 55th Division at Martaban, which had fought in the campaign from start to finish under General

Yiroshi Takaeuchi. It was thought by General Iida, commanding the 15th Army, to be too slow in its advance and lacking in aggression; it received no congratulations for what it had done in the early stages of the invasion of Burma, when success against poorly organised opposition was considered not to have been followed up quickly enough. General Takaeuchi was retired in 1943.

The only comparable unit to 33rd Division on the British-Indian side was 7th Armoured Brigade, two tank regiments armed with Stuart tanks and two batteries of guns commanded throughout by Brigadier Anstice. Their officers, tank crews, maintenance and support staff, as well as their gunners, were comparable to the experienced Japanese, and their performance can be assessed by the same military standards because they had already seen considerable action in the Western Desert, Libya, and were used to functioning as a unit. The other British and Indian units and the Burmese units, which were usually made up of hill men and locally recruited Indians and Gurkhas, had no experience of modern warfare and had only participated in small-scale manoeuvres. These had usually been carried out in the cool season – the average day-time heat at the end of the campaign was 100 degrees Fahrenheit (38°C). They would have been deployed as dispersed companies in support of the civil administration, as for example during the 1938 Rangoon riots, which may have been the trigger for their distrust of the Burmese. It is not imputing any lack of bravery or effort to state that their officers and men were not comparable to the Japanese. The senior officers had had experience as junior officers in World War I with some having had experience of anti-guerrilla fighting in the arid mountain conditions of the North-West Frontier. A few of the British infantry may have had experience in France and Norway, but that would not have had much relevance to what they were about to endure.

The British-Indian side had long lamented the absence of adequate equipment in both quantity and quality but the Japanese thought it better than their own. 33 Division came over the mountains dividing Burma from Thailand on foot and were seriously under-equipped by British-Indian standards; they improvised brilliantly using captured equipment whenever available. The speed of their advance was dictated more by the extent of physical exhaustion of their men rather than by any equipment shortage. The Japanese marched as a matter of course and not as the result of enforced retreat. They appeared to be able to keep up this level of effort on what the British would consider to be inadequate rations.

The Japanese staff work was good, as was the British and Indian, without which their forces would not have been able to retreat for so long and over such an enormous distance without any previous training, coping with an eroding sequence of minor defeats. This aspect of the retreat has not received the level of praise that it perhaps should have: the Japanese made do with less because that was the way that they had been taught to function in war, while the British-Indian staff had been trained to expect far more and was forced to function very little – and in fact did it extraordinarily well.

Ian Hamilton, who subsequently failed as a general in the Dardanelles, was military attaché in Japan at the time of the Russo-Japanese War in 1905. He had noted the high morale and fighting spirit of the Japanese infantry and how they administered to their own wounded effectively. His report was filed away as not relevant to the current political climate and ignored by most. The British did not know what they were facing, despite the earlier warnings. Even when he was in Mission 204 in Maymyo at the the Bush Warfare School, preparing to enter China to give some token support to the Chinese prior to Pearl Harbor and the start of the Japanese war, Ralph Tanner cannot remember anything more than being shown a chart of Japanese badges of rank, and yet there were officers on site who had previously held commercial positions in China. The training he remembers was 'playing about' with anti-tank grenades of dubious efficacy and blowing up embankments.

To miss out of the training of officers the fact that the Japanese Army was both aggressive and professionally competent and well able to function with very little administrative support was certainly a serious failure.

The savagery of the Japanese soldiers in Burma was something that developed well before World War II, and once it became known to British and Indian troops it was mirrored by them in their attitude towards both the enemy and Burmese civilians of doubtful loyalty. They had perhaps no alternative owing to prolonged fear and uncertainty, once Japanese behaviour in Hong Kong became known to every soldier. There was a religious factor in Japanese morale since they shared with other Eastern people a belief in karmic rebirth.

Conversations with Japanese officers who had served in Burma after the War showed that they themselves thought that they had been too brutal to their own men and that their care of the wounded and sick was incomparably poor in comparison to British-Indian care. The Japanese had no channel to public opinion which could have led to a demand for better attention to be paid to the welfare of their soldiers, as resulted in Britain after William Russell's reports on the appalling inefficiency of staff work in the Crimean War had been published in *The Times*. It is in retrospect perhaps surprising that the Battalion escaped so often from the deadly momentum of the experienced Japanese, dominant in the jungle and in the air, where it counted in Burma – it must be attributed to the bravery and adaptive skills of these Yorkshiremen. But at the beginning of the campaign, they had yet to learn that 'the individual Japanese soldier [was] the most formidable fighting insect in history' (Slim 1956: 381).

Training

There were fundamental differences between the two military systems in how they trained their infantry for war and the ideologies behind that training. In Japan the Army had adopted a political role that was to a large extent independent of civilian control, so from the early 1930s the Army trained their men with war immediately in their minds. They developed methods of ideological training that made their infantry effective even in the absence of equipment, which the Allies had in massive quantities. The Army – and indeed all the services – had a devotion to the Emperor as the background to all their training, although the Emperor in the Japanese historical tradition was a figurehead, with real power elsewhere.

The Japanese Army was trained for war without much attention paid to the maintenance of unit morale, which was compensated for by the constant repetition of ceremonies highlighting devotion to the Emperor. An eighty-page training pamphlet entitled 'Read this and we will win' was issued to every soldier involved in southern operations, in which the second chapter is headed 'Obey the will of the Emperor' and ends with 'We will carry forward our glorious 2,600-year-old history and in accordance with the trust place in us by His Majesty the Commander-in-Chief, embark upon the honourable duty of changing the course of world history ... The completion of the Showa Restoration's aim to free Asia, which is the desire of His Imperial Majesty, rests upon our shoulders.'[8]

Loyalty to the Crown was part of the swearing in of new British recruits but other than the annual King's Birthday parade, there was nothing to compare with the Japanese continual reminders of loyalty to the Emperor. The Union Jack was flown beside the Battalion Headquarters but it never had the same ritual importance that the Stars and Stripes had and has for the armed forces of the United States. The parade for Minden Day in memory of an earlier regimental battle distinction and the regimental colours were probably of more immediate significance to the men of 2/KOYLI than their national affiliations.

The Japanese army had no shortage of men. There was two years national service and the men were organised into units with regional attachments. It was certainly not a peasant army, their literacy rate was higher than that of the Indian Army. They were formidable and made so by their training, devoted to the preparation for war, and in many cases by their combat experience in China and along the Manchurian frontier with Russia. The Allies certainly underestimated their fighting abilities and the quality of their staff work, in part because of the underlying racist bias that Asians could only be turned into competent soldiers when led by Europeans.

How did the preparations of the 2/KOYLI compare to what the Japanese were doing? In all fairness there can be no comparison at all because their training was not geared towards war in Asia. The British Army saw their role in India and Burma as to enforce the will of the civil government and prevent a repetition of the 1857 Indian Mutiny; and in Burma a recurrence of the Saya San rebellion of 1935. They were also there to prevent the ever-present possibility of conflict between Burmans and Indians, the latter hated because of their success in trade and their acquisition of Burmese land from loan indebtedness.

This Battalion was not preparing for war unless in Europe or perhaps the Western Desert. There was limited training for riot control. The annual manoeuvres in good weather were not much more than play acting, without any stress on long-term physical endurance. There was nothing approaching what the American forces had instituted after the end of World War I, monthly exercises with no warning, during which each 'emergency' was planned to test different reactions. In the short time between Pearl Harbor and the onset of hostilities there was no time to develop new training methods before the baptism of fire.

The British commanding officers had memories of World War I to the fore and this would have been France rather than

German East Africa, or Palestine. Similarly, the local planners would have been hoping for the use of the Battalion in Libya rather than Italian East Africa, which had already been conquered. The officers, as professional soldiers, wanted to fight the Germans rather than sitting out the War in Burma. Few spent their time learning the local language or Urdu, the lingua franca of the Indian Army; in the lull before the storm they were more likely enjoying regimental sports such as golf or tennis. They would have had plenty of spare time since most of their military duties would have finished by midday. While a few of the soldiers may have had a spattering of military Urdu, only the few Anglo-Burmans recruited by the Battalion would have had any knowledge of Burmese and they were worth their weight in gold as the campaign progressed.

No training can replicate actual warfare. No one has disputed that the Battalion when it was mobilised was fit by the existing standards of British infantry; but it was a fitness related to the environment of Maymyo on the edge of the Shan States, at an altitude producing a climate similar to an English spring. Route marches for these men would have been long enough, but they knew where the end was going to be. They did not replicate Wingate's training schedules for the second incursion in which, on apparently completing a training march, the men were told that rest, food and water were only available at the place from which they had started. General Wingate based his training programme on the extraordinary harshness of the first Chindit incursion into upper Burma (Fergusson 1946). He made training for the second Chindit incursion as unpredictable and arduous as possible, particularly as his units were made up of ordinary soldiers and not ones specially selected for long-range penetration of enemy territory on foot. Some of Wavell's pre-war training exercises at Aldershot had this element of unpredictability built into them, no doubt to the dismay of the orthodox planners of field exercises. Field training for this Battalion was at Kangyi, another Shan State site and the 1937 photographs show white tents in lines. Whatever these men did in their field exercises it was not adequate preparation for the humid forested areas of southern Burma and no preparation at all for the largely waterless areas of central Burma, with rock-hard ground into which they would have to dig slit-trenches.

The Battalion as a closed society

Those joining the King's Own Yorkshire Light Infantry would soon know of its initial success at the battle of Minden without knowing anything about that ancient war, they would learn of the battle honours on the regimental colours and that the Queen was their Colonel-in-Chief. This may not seem much but it certainly built up into a feeling of regimental exclusivity, not only in relation to civilians but also to other infantry regiments; in the words of John Heald in a letter to Ralph Tanner, 'Once a KOYLI always a KOYLI'. Soldiers who throughout the war transferred between units can never have gained this intense feeling of commitment to a particular regiment. This Battalion, like all others, had a fixed hierarchy based on written rules, within which promotion was by tests, long service and through personal recommendation. Everyone was full-time and salaried and their separate responsibilities were well defined; in fact it was a structure which could be said almost inevitably to block the initiatives necessary for adapting to the uncertainties of this kind of war.

This formal structure was however consistently modified by an informal structure running parallel to its bureaucracy: the sophisticated manipulation of regulations which all soldiers of whatever rank learned from their first encounters with the military as recruits. At the higher level there were personal connections between officers who had known each other for many years and lower down – accumulated cunning. Quartermasters particularly, achieved flexibility by unofficial tinkering with formal rules, and long service senior NCOs were invaluable in their understanding of what could be hidden and what should be disclosed; their more sensible officers would come to rely on them. Once the Battalion went overseas in 1919 this same structure was of course in a more isolated environment. Back home when men were off-duty or on leave they more or less disappeared into the outside world. Once overseas, officers could go on local leave to places which provided equivalent accommodation to their quarters in Maymyo's Alexandra Barracks. The men on the other hand could not afford to do this, so the Battalion arranged for leave 'holiday' camps in other parts of the Shan States where they were relatively free of military discipline.

These men in Burma, even before the Japanese invasion, felt cut off, if not forgotten. They knew that they were foreigners in a foreign country and with their limited money they often preferred to stay in barracks and use the canteen than to go down town for egg and chips at the Salvation Army. Sport became more important than it might have been in Britain. Emotional support tended to come from within the Battalion and not from anything or anyone outside the barracks, which was two miles away from the town. The Battalion thus came to have the characteristics of an extended family in which everyone knew a lot about everyone else and from whom they gained support. Certainly there were tensions but there was no return in letting them surface too obviously because everyone had to continue to live in close proximity. There were other, quite literal, family connections. We do not know how many men followed their fathers or brothers into the regiment, but it must have been quite a number; the current Regimental Secretary followed his father and grandfather into the regiment. In the surviving roll of those who served in the Battalion in Burma in 1942 there were fourteen sets of brothers and three from one family. Ralph Tanner recalls, for example, the death of the Mooney twins, but the Commonwealth War Graves Commission has no record of their deaths.

In this same roll at least 45 men and one officer were listed with their nicknames, suggesting close camaraderie remembered over a lapse of years. Only a few were married and they tended to be the older officers and men; one had to be over 26 and the number who could get the permission of the commanding officer to marry would have been limited by the quarters available. It seems certain that to marry locally would have been heavily discouraged, seen as complicating professional and social arrangements. So this Battalion, socially isolated in Burma, depended much more on itself, more indeed than one serving in India, where there was likely to be more than one British battalion not too far off for competitive sport, as well as hill stations in which there would have been some leave facilities for other ranks.

Women and children

The men of the battalion did not have their women and children with them, but knew that their next of kin were among their own friends and family and neighbours, and rationally they had no need to worry over their safety; the government would see that they were cared for. There was only the plain misery of separation shared by all soldiers, from loved ones and simply from female company of any kind. Ralph Tanner worked out that in the two years overseas to the end of the Burma campaign and being invalided out from India – other than nurses in the hospitals in which he spent some months – he had spoken to not more than three women in a non-military setting. There were only about 35 married men and two married officers at the start of the Japanese war. Locally born men of mixed parentage were on occasions recruited – Corporal Howson who earned the Military Medal for bravery was an example – and some men had relationships which were started locally; two men are recorded as having married local women and there may have been others.

When Ralph Tanner was the escorting officer in early March 1942 for the evacuation of the Battalion's wives and children from Magwe by air,[9] he remembers that besides the British, there was one young Burmese wife in Burmese dress nursing a baby and an older, tall Hindu woman in a sari. (But the son of Regimental-Sergeant-Major Delaney who was in the same convoy aged 13 years had no memory of such women.)

Even allowing for the pleasant climate of Maymyo and the town not being too far away, there would have been no diversions comparable to those available on their doorstep in Pontefract or Strensall. Many men must have sought female companionship and some might well have made semi-permanent relationships with local women.

As the Battalion mobilised for war it moved to Takaw in the Southern Shan States, leaving a small detachment of the sick, never to return, except for those in the first half of the campaign who came back sick or wounded. The men with wives, children or local relationships would have realised soon enough that the safety of their loved ones depended on what the regimental headquarters could arrange, since the civil government had collapsed and would never have accepted responsibility for military families. For their sweethearts, the safest option was to appear as Burmese and un-Indian as possible. They would have known, from gossip and the experience of the older soldiers in the Rangoon riots of 1938, the savagery of which the Burmese men were capable, and that at best the Burmese were passively hostile to the British. The anxieties of men about their wives and children would have added substantially to the worries of the campaign and this was even more grave because these men would have been almost all of the senior NCOs and those recently commissioned; the most experienced men in the

Battalion. When did they know that their wives and children were safe in India? At what stage did the recently married Major Wardleworth find out that his wife had been killed on Myitkyina airfield, as the cargo plane in which she was a passenger was taking off?

British equipment

It has already been suggested that the Japanese were not as well equipped as the British and Indian troops which they were attacking and that they were aware of this as soon as they had captured equipment and turned it to their own use. The British captured enormous quantities if Italian equipment in Libya and Ethiopia in 1940–1 but did not use it in front line service as it was found to be inferior. No unit, however well prepared materially and physically, enters a campaign fully equipped with the men and material to which it was entitled in the regulations; there are always accidents and breakdowns and personnel go sick. The Battalion was short of the equipment required for infantry operations based on the roads and even more so for operations off-road, involving more than one river to cross. It was probably adequately equipped for a few days of operations in support of the civil power. More importantly, it was probably two hundred men below its war-time establishment and had been milked of some experienced officers and senior NCOs who had been sent home in 1939.

This left the Battalion short of experienced men who knew the soldiers under their command and were known to them, and left companies short of the psychological cohesion necessary when things go wrong. 2nd Lieut. Ableson was killed two days after joining the battalion from a draft of new officers and it is doubtful if anyone involved with him even knew his name.[10]

What were the deficiencies in equipment at the moment of the move to Takaw? They probably had enough picks and shovels to dig when all was quiet but they had no entrenching tools for digging in under fire. The Battalion had only six 15 cwt trucks, which would have been adequate for no more than six platoons, let alone a whole battalion, and there is no mention that they were provided with any mules or mule carts until much later on. They had four three-inch mortars but no two-inch ones, which were more mobile, and their Vickers medium machine-guns shown in 1937 photographs had been taken away to be used by other units and never replaced. Most serious was the lack of wirelesses, leaving them reliant on messengers; this meant that sometimes – as at Toksan – the message never arrived. Messages were on occasion dropped from an aircraft on a hit or miss basis. A formal picture of the Battalion's signallers in 1937 shows them with white signalling flags and telescopes, adequate in the conditions of the North-West Frontier or performing practice manoeuvres in open country, but of severely limited practicability in forested terrain.

There is a psychological factor in equipment inadequacy. The men must have known that what they were going to war with was out-of-date even in comparison to that which was available in Britain after Dunkirk. They knew it was out-of-date when compared with German materiel and as the campaign progressed they garnered the feeling that the Japanese equipment must also be better. What was the point in the Battalion having a single Boyes anti-tank rifle, which was probably only capable of penetrating the armour of a Bren carrier? The men had to make do with what they had. So much depended on ingenuity and strength of character.

Racism

The final British weakness was their overall attitude to the society in which they found themselves and which they were supposed to protect, as well as their assessment of the enemy.

It would not have been any different to that of any occupying army, however benignly they construed their roles and however much they deluded themselves into thinking that they were, if not liked, at least tolerated. These soldiers thought themselves superior to civilian Indians but accepted that the Indian Army had some military qualities equal to their own, and they were more suspicious of Hindus than Muslims or Sikhs. Their affection was mainly reserved for the Gurkhas. After their experience of the Burmese killing of Indian civilians in the Rangoon 1938 riots their sympathies would have been more with the Indians, despite Indian civilian hostility to the Battalion in the Peshawar riots of 1930. Leaving aside any element of racism, endemic in the British Army, the experience of those soldiers remaining in the Battalion who had seen civilian unrest first-hand would have made newcomers very much aware of a general dislike or distrust of 'native' civilians.

Finally there was the quite extraordinary feeling of superiority to the Japanese. Ralph Tanner remembers well enough – as do many others – being told that the Japanese could not fly warplanes because they all had poor eye-sight and that they were only copiers of what Westerners had invented; after all, they had not even succeeded in beating the Chinese. No one remembered their victory in the Russo-Japanese war of 1905 – and the fact that they had started that war without the diplomatic formalities of a declaration. This Battalion, through no clear fault of its own, or indeed of its commanders, was prepared for a type of warfare that did not exist in Asia.

Chapter 3

Into Action

The Salween at Takaw

The Battalion mobilised in August 1941 and moved to Taungdwingyi, the centre of the Southern Shan States and the area's only town, situated in rolling, open country. It was on the only road from Thazi, on the Rangoon to Mandalay railway to Chiang-mai railhead in Thailand, which crossed the Salween at Takaw on a wire-held ferry of one 3-ton lorry capacity. The Battalion was the only unit that Burma Command could use to counter anticipated Japanese incursion. Tied mentally to the use of road and rail, the British guessed that the Japanese, if they came at all, would not choose to come over the mountains on foot, over tracks which led more directly to Rangoon. This was before the crisis point with the United States had been reached.

In December they moved to Loilem, further down the road but still in open country and then immediately after Pearl Harbor to Takaw, the ferry point over the Salween, a fast-flowing river through a gorge 800 ft above sea level, surrounded on either side with 7000 ft mountains with no cultivatable flood plains, and consequently, no villages. With the help of some five hundred local workers, defensive positions were constructed and demolitions prepared for several miles on both sides of the river. It was a gloomy, miserable place in which the sun only hit the road cuttings at midday. No one lived there.

Malaria hit the Battalion badly. In 1939, with a population of 16.8 million, there were 600,000 hospitalisations for malaria in Burma; in India there were considerably more than 1 million deaths. While the first infected went back to Maymyo, this led to such a shortage of men that the medical officer established a local field hospital a few miles back so that men could return to duty earlier. This was long before mepacrine was available. The Japanese do not seem to have taken much notice of malaria and did not accept it as a reason for leaving front line duty. The Battalion's experience of Takaw must have been a miserable one, with monotonous work in an unpleasant environment. The diminished Battalion was relieved to be ordered south to Moulmein.

The Japanese crossing of the Salween

By the time that the Battalion had reached southern Burma, Moulmein had already fallen and the small force was tasked with defending a river front of over twenty miles with a single brigade. (Moulmein had been a mess, indefensible without reinforcements and the delay in redeploying the KOYLI inexcusable. As the Battalion arrived at Thaton, the garrison was disembarking from ferries at Martaban on the far bank of the Salween.) Steeped in the ideas of more settled warfare, to the men and their officers there was a front and soldiers went up to it from bases of some stability. There was in fact never any stability in any front, nor continuous occupation of a line. As the original campaign maps show, the British-Indian positions were isolated red blobs on the enormous expanse of Burma and the Japanese, indicated by blue arrows, moved into gaps where the British-Indian forces were either positioned in small numbers or simply not there at all. The Battalion stopped at Hninpale, a village just short of Thaton twenty miles from the Salween crossing at Martaban and on the railway line.

The Battalion's introduction to the realities of war were train loads of wounded and the disorganised human detritus of war passing through. They became aware of the breakdown of civil administration, sharpening their anxieties over their families and friends in Maymyo. The legacy of the stay at Takaw started to make itself felt, with 200 cases of malaria relapses.

With such a long river front to cover it was inevitable that the Battalion was split up. D Company was sent to Martaban, which was being bombed and shelled daily, with orders to stay there until they received further instructions. The inevitable happened in the absence of wireless, the Brigade's order for them to retire was never received and when their commander decided to move back they had to abandon everything which they could not carry, faced with a long and extremely hard march of about fifty miles to Thaton across country, away from the roads and railway. With Martaban in their hands, the Japanese controlled the Salween estuary and could land troops at will.

A Company was up-stream at Kuzeik opposite Paan and lost all the Battalion's mule transport when they were sent with supplies up to the Baluchis to the north, who were attacked almost as soon as they arrived. The Japanese crossed the river at Hmawbwi and established a roadblock eight miles north of Martaban. The Battalion stayed five miles south of Thaton on the far side of this road block for four days. So the first experience of war was defeat, dispersal – which meant they had not acted as the unit with which they felt accustomed – the loss of equipment, and first casualties. A miserable business: ineffectual opposition to the Japanese with nothing to show for it.

The Bilin fiasco

While the Salween at Moulmein was a formidable barrier, the Bilin as the next river along the line withdrawal was no barrier at all and was no more than knee deep; it could be crossed wherever the Japanese should choose. The Battalion was the last to leave Thaton and in doing so had to abandon its stores, as the train which was supposed to carry them and the stores back did not arrive until some time after they had decided to start marching; the first of many losses that could never be replaced. It was now part of 16 Brigade, which had to cover a 15-mile front along the shallow river, as well as keeping an eye on the seaboard side of the road and railway on which the Japanese could just as easily have landed using the boats they had captured at Moulmein. B Company was posted at Yinon eight miles upstream, where it was out of sight and in terms of possible support was more or less out of mind. D Company was at Danyingon with the Headquarters company and the weakened and only partially rested A Company were positioned on a prominent hill half a mile to the north.

During that day both groups were attacked repeatedly by the Japanese and suffered as well as caused numerous casualties. Eventually, the isolated company at Yinon was ordered to retire by a message dropped from the air onto open ground in front of their position, telling them to abandon all their heavy equipment. Prior to this order they had been heavily bombed and machine-gunned by both Japanese and Allied aircraft (the British and the American Volunteer Group were unmistakable, with sharks painted on the noses of their fighters). The Battalion had been able to dig shallow slit trenches with their bayonets and there were no serious casualties, which suggests that the effect of the air attacks was more psychological than actual. To hide under a bush from an aircraft flying at 2000 feet is not sensible and is a sign of diminishing morale. At Bilin, at least the Japanese were brought to a temporary halt by resistance they had not experienced so far in Burma.

This was the first time in this campaign that the Japanese had come up against British infantry and General Iida noted the strong British resistance (Grant and Tamayama 1999: 100-01). The official history of 114 regiment commented that the Japanese were surprised by the huge volume of British small arms fire, which they had never previously experienced or imagined, as the Japanese Army had always stressed the importance of conservation of ammunition. Following this first encounter they began to learn to outflank and attack from the rear, and at night.

After this action the depleted Battalion had to march back towards the Sittang bridge over the wide river.

The Sittang Bridge disaster

With most wireless equipment lost or destroyed and only available at Brigade level anyway, the order to blow the 500-metre railway bridge – which had just been adapted to take wheeled transport – was almost inevitably going to be acted upon too early (as in this case, according to some, but not all, commentators) or too late. General Davies later commented on General John Smyth's dilemma: 'A terrible decision had to be made … If he [Smyth] blew the bridge he sacrificed the bulk of his division. If he failed to blow the bridge and it was secured intact by the enemy, the way to Rangoon lay open with nothing interposing. General Smyth blew the bridge. In my opinion a heroic and inevitable decision.' (*Milestones* Smyth: 190).

The bridge was blown at 0530 on Monday 23 February, with two brigades on the far, eastern side. All their irreplaceable equipment was lost and the men had to swim for it. All the boats had been taken to the western bank to prevent them being used by the Japanese. Not all the soldiers could swim and those that could were exhausted after many days of hardship;

and this was a wide, deep river. The initial plan had been to cross at night but the Japanese pressure meant that the attempt was made in the afternoon. 2/KOYLI fought alongside 8 BURIF, 3/7 Gurkhas and 5/15 Dogras through the day. It is estimated that six officers and two hundred men from 2/KOYLI crossed, most that night, but they would have now been bootless and probably only in their shorts.

Some would have been picked up within a few miles but the majority had to walk the 25 miles to Waw, where Smyth had relocated HQ on the day the bridge was blown, through the middle of the day. When the sick and wounded of the Battalion were deducted, the total strength of the battalion was now no more than eighty all ranks. So before the end of February the Battalion had ceased to exist in terms of numbers of men and equipment; a battalion in name only – and it still had a long way to go before reaching India at the end of May.

The Battalion was situated north of the Japanese roadblock that had been formed on the main Mandalay-Pegu-Rangoon road to stop reinforcements reaching Rangoon, which the Japanese assumed would be defended by the British. In fact, the city had been evacuated by the Burma Army and its headquarters, which could not pass the roadblock. Fortunately for the Allies, the Japanese miscalculated British intentions and moved off the roadblock, sending two regiments south to attack Rangoon. The Battalion was bypassed by these Japanese columns, which were seen and heard by the listening posts, and no more casualties were suffered other than those incurred when they had approached the roadblocks earlier. They were able to get away to Yenangyaung and relative quiet.

The failure to withdraw at Toksan

At Yenangyaung the Battalion rested for a week and reformed itself into something resembling a battalion by getting some men back from the Maymyo depot and hospital, where they had been recovering from wounds, malaria and other illnesses. It also had some of its heavy equipment replaced, gaining a few 3-inch mortars and two Vickers machine-guns. From an upstairs window, Ralph saw General Alexander arriving to visit the Battalion at Yenangyaung. He does not know what went on between Alexander and Colonel Chadwick and was told nothing, even though he was sharing a room with Major Martin, the Adjutant. Harold Alexander had arrived in Rangoon on 5 March, too late to save the city. In the words of Churchill: '... if we could not send an army, we could at any rate send a man.'

The Battalion still only had a total of some three hundred men, enough to form four understrength rifle companies – in fact no more than strong platoons – and an even weaker HQ company. It moved first to Thityagauk (Maps 8 and 9) south of the Yin Chaung. Other units had retreated behind its shallow running water after some serious fighting at Migyaungyee on the Irrawaddy. Reacting to Japanese encroachment it moved to Toksan (Map 10) leaving the transport with the mortars and mules to follow on. It was heavily attacked soon after dawn and after a counter-attack moved to a position less overlooked. In this action the transport and heavy equipment was lost yet again, as well as a number of men killed and wounded. The order to retire had been sent but the officer carrying it was thrown from his horse and injured and attempts to flash a message from the river in Morse code were unsuccessful.

As listening posts reported Japanese movements all round, the Battalion moved back at night in single file, undoubtedly passing through Japanese parties lying up for the night round their cooking fires; a nerve-shredding march. When the Battalion reached Magwe it was down to two hundred men and with no equipment other than what the men were carrying. After more than a day without water the only relief from their miseries was wading through the Yin Chaung, even though they were fired on by Indian troops on the way, who were nervous about being deceived by Japanese calling out in English, which had happened to them elsewhere.

The oilfield inferno at Yenangyaung

From Magwe the Battalion was first moved out onto the Taungdwingyi road by lorry, where it was shelled (Map 11). It then had to march across country to the Yenangyaung oilfields (photos 12 and 24). It was the objective of the Japanese 33rd Division to move up the eastern side of the Irrawaddy and capture the oilfields intact to secure the all-important fuel. The whole of the Burma Army, men, lorries, tanks and guns, became bottled up in the small area of the oilfields to the south of the shallow-watered Pin Chaung, an area of about twenty square miles, on the far side of which the Japanese had established a roadblock. The bare, rocky ravines were without shade and quite waterless, with a daytime temperature above 100 degrees, and with the oil tank farm on fire this was an infernal place in which no one would have chosen to spend two minutes, much less two days.

The Battalion had to just sit and hope, but it at least had an issue of water, when an Indian engineer company sucked water out of the Yenangyaung club swimming pool after the pumping station on the Irrawaddy had been blown up. On 15 April, the whole oilfield complex was blown up. By the next day the Japanese had infiltrated the 'suburbs', having landed from launches on the river side of the town. Something like 7,000 soldiers and hundreds of civilians were surrounded. There was no food, ammunition was low, and most debilitating of all in that inferno, practically no more drinking water. The Chinese Army that had come down from Yunnan and performed well in attacking the Japanese at Toungoo, finally cleared the roadblock in pyrotechnic style (Map 5). This allowed some of the transport to get out. Though this was after another escape route had been found, a track a mile or so upstream that led to the Pin Chaung. The soft-skinned vehicles that took this route would be abandoned in the soft sand once the banks of the Pin Chaung were reached, and any wounded that could not be transferred to the tanks were left behind, later reportedly to be butchered by the enemy.

The Battalion had been told to make its own way out, the men moving independently round Twinggone, which was also occupied by the Japanese, crossing the Pin Chaung with relief (photo 13) and going beyond the roadblock where they were picked up by lorries and taken to Mount Popa (Map 16) where they had fresh water, cool air and green trees. 1 BUR DIV had been more or less destroyed as a fighting force at Yenangyaung; though this did not mean they did not fight with distinction and determination two weeks later at Monywa. The Battalion's numbers were now down to about 150 (Photo 16). See maps 12, 13, 14, 15.

Taungtha and crossing the Irrawaddy river to Monywa

The Battalion were transported to Taungtha, to wait at a crossroads for the last of the Chinese to come through to join the main body, which was moving north on a line independent of the British-Indian line to India, via Kalewa on the Chindwin river and Tamu. It stayed there some time. During this period some twenty or so supposed looters were shot by volunteers. This became the subject of a Scotland Yard investigation in the 1970s. Ralph was interviewed by two detectives about this suspected war crime some forty years after the event, investigated eventually because of ill-judged remarks to a local paper by the officer involved. All that can be said in mitigation of this incident must be that, in Ralph Tanner's words in the diary, frightened men with guns are profligate in their use. Retreats are emotionally exhausting and in addition to fear of the enemy, there is the fear of the civil population hanging around the fringes of the line of march waiting to pick up abandoned equipment and maybe pick off stragglers. Most survivors had some experience of this. On the other hand, Ralph was fed by Burmese south of Magwe, where they could just as easily have killed him. The Battalion foraged in the abandoned houses and would have found plenty of palm juice sugar lumps to give them an energy boost.

Next stop was Myingyan (Map 17) a large town which was totally deserted, with some structures burning. These were probably Indian-owned rice mills. The Battalion bivouacked in fields beyond the houses and it started to rain, but everyone was too tired to notice. Following this the men were taken by lorry to Sameikkon and crossed the Irrawaddy in fine style in motor boats manned by a detachment of the Royal Marines, without any interdiction from the air. But then it was marching again across country with the expectation of being lifted by boats up the Chindwin river and then to march across country to Tamu. Slim had intended to move 1 Bur Brigade and 13th Indian by truck to Monywa, but it will come as no surprise that there were none available. As soon as the Battalion had got within earshot of Monywa it was obvious that the Japanese had got there first (Map 18) and in force; again using captured boats, as well as some of their own landing craft, which had come up river from Rangoon on ships coming round from Singapore. The Japanese Navy had gained control of the Bay of Bengal after the remnants of the Royal Navy East had retired to East Africa following the sinkings off Singapore. Since the Japanese could not be dislodged – despite the efforts of 1 Bur Brigade and and 13th Brigade to retake the town on 2 May – the Battalion crept round well clear of Monywa in the dark, on village tracks. Again, it was partially lifted by transport along the main road to Yeu as far as the turn off to Kalewa, along a sandy winding track described on the map as motorable in the dry season. But the first showers of the coming monsoon had already fallen. At the turn off there were piles of rations and a chalked notice board told everyone to take what they could carry. They were then lifted some part of the way to Pyingaing.

The cut across country

The next halt was in open teak forest at Pyingaing where the men had to dig for water and collect firewood (Photo 17). From then on I Bur Brigade, which in practice cannot have numbered enough men to make up even a weak battalion, struck north, first along jungle tracks. Pencil lines on the map mark where the battalion halted, with each battalion taking the lead in turn as the path was cleared enough for the few mules to get through with their loads (Photos 18 and 19). They dug for water at bends in dried out ravines. After three days they reached the small abandoned oilfield at Indaw where they had optimistically been told there was a chance of getting transport, but there was none, just a few abandoned houses. They pressed on along the river to the Chindwin The Brigade crossed the Chindwin river at Yuwa after an exhausting night march and then went over the mountain ridge and down into Tamu, where the Brigadier was told that they had arrived too soon and they should have stayed out to the east in case the Japanese had followed them up.

The Battalion had to march five miles south through forest stinking of dead refugees. The next day they were lifted to Imphal where the monsoon had started. They got there just in time. 'I will lift my eyes unto the mountains. From whence shall my help come?'

James Lunt in *A Hell of a Licking* tells the story of how author Bernard Fergusson, commenting on Alexander's choice of the route for the retreat many years later, pointed out to him that any student at the Staff College who had decided upon it would have been immediately returned to his unit for proposing anything so crazy. But the alternative – from Mogaung or Myitkyina through the Hukawng valley to Ledo in Assam – was even worse: dauntingly steep and almost impassable to vehicles.

Chapter 4

A Reckoning

Japanese behaviour

There can be no doubt at all that the war with Japan was fought with exceptional barbarism; and as far as the British-Indian soldiers were concerned this began almost from the first days, after the British learned how the Japanese soldiers had behaved in Hong Kong before the end of December 1941 towards the nurses and the wounded in hospital. The knowledge of this behaviour was common to all ranks but not publicly expressed by senior officers.

Up to this time the war with Germany had been, by and large, conducted along acceptable lines. There were some exceptions of course but the comments, if any, were about the German Army's effectiveness, not its barbarism; the soldiers facing the British were not then known to have been killing hostages in Crete. In crude terms, it was a war between Europeans more or less according to the rules and implied customs of war which they had themselves created. There was no widespread hatred of the Germans.

In the earlier and first modern war between Asians and Europeans, the Russo-Japanese War of 1905–7, the Japanese army behaved in ways that produced few complaints and certainly no suggestion of barbarism. As mentioned earlier,

Sir Ian Hamilton as military attaché was present in the field and wrote favourably about their behaviour and their treatment of prisoners. Later historians (Lone 1998) have confirmed this, stating that the seventy thousand Russian prisoners were treated well and there were suggestions in the Japanese press that some did not want to be repatriated. Also, there does not seem to have been any military or civilian accusation that disgrace attached to the two thousand Japanese soldiers who were captured by the Russians.

So there can be little doubt that the barbarity of the Japanese Army developed in the 1930s as a result of the invasion of China, the experience of guerrilla warfare, and the dominance of the Army in politics. (The Japanese Navy and Air Forces were not involved with civilian populations.)

It was a fact that members of KOYLI feared Japanese behaviour as likely to be beyond anything which they might perpetrate themselves. This was separate to their appreciation of Japanese military expertise and doggedness, which they feared in quite a different way and perhaps reluctantly admired.

The misbehaviour of British soldiers

Many institutions, whether schools, companies, government departments or military units, have two codes of conduct: the overt behaviour required by the institution, which it endeavours to supervise and enforce, and a covert code which carries on parallel to the official one, which is a response to official bureaucracy and often an expression of creative individuality. Soldiers, according to their length of service become experts in following the rules, so that good conduct stripes are earned as the reward for years of undetected 'crime'. Non-commissioned officers know what is going on and do their best to ensure that it is kept within reasonable bounds. Officers do not want to know the details and see the meta-code as a necessary part of keeping the battalion machinery working and contributing to morale. The most ingenious manipulators of the rules are the quartermasters who it might be said have two sets of accounts.

Soldiers are invariably light fingered and always manage to acquire, especially under field conditions, the little extras that make life easier. Fraser has written a delightful account of how a section of the Border Regiment (Fraser 1992: 97-103) collected considerable extra supplies for their own use at an air-drop site near Meiktila in 1944. This incident happened at a time when the British-Indian army was at the peak of its power, and this pilfering was undertaken to show their individual and section superiority over officialdom as well as to make themselves a little more comfortable in the dangerous days ahead. This was not quite stealing and could not be defined as looting. In warfare, and particularly in retreat, the rules are increasingly ignored as conditions get worse. The Quartermaster at Yenangyaung wanted to take the crockery from the houses in which the Battalion was billeted as they left, but the Colonel forbade this, as he said that subsequent units would want to use it. There were, however, no following units, and the men of the Battalion were stuck with their mess tins and spoons. Since they could only take what they could carry, what was taken by the Battalion was confined to what it really needed along the line of march.

It has been suggested that in April 1942 members of KOYLI shot 17 Burmese villagers because they suspected them of giving away their position to the Japanese. The reaction of James Lunt in his book *A Hell of a Licking* to this unprovable allegation is pertinent. It was, he writes '... if true, a nasty business, but none of us who fought in that campaign will cast a single stone. For there were similar incidents, without any doubt. The cold hard fury of the Cameronians when they found their bayoneted comrades; the 'Dukes' who found their popular commanding officer with his throat cut, after accepting Burmese hospitality. The Marines bayoneted to death after the raid on Henzada; the Indians maimed, raped, slaughtered in their thousands by gangs of bloodthirsty Burmese ruffians.'

Accidental losses

The tragic cases of friendly fire, or blue on blue in modern parlance, are far more frequent that those involved would like to admit. This is more likely to happen in mobile warfare than in more static confrontations, but even then, shells drop short. At Danyingon there was a report that 3-inch mortar bombs fell short on a platoon out in the open. At Bilin, the Battalion was both bombed and machine-gunned by the RAF and American Volunteer Group but the regimental history goes no further than to record that there were very few casualties. At Toksan, RSM Bootland was shot in the throat while trying to drive away a lorry on which there were Burmese. But the suggestion that he was shot deliberately by one of his own men in such a confused situation simply because he was the Regimental Sergeant Major and so had made enemies is no more than idle speculation.

One soldier fell down a well and drowned before his absence was noticed; and of course some drowned trying to cross the Sittang because they could not swim and could not find anything on the far side which could have kept them afloat. The most tragic accident occurred at Taungtha, when Major Martin and three others, finding a cinema stacked with supplies, attempted to destroy it because it would have fallen into the hands of the enemy. They used petrol and on setting fire to it from outside, they were all burnt by a gush of flames coming out of the door. All four died of their burns later and have no known grave.

The process of attrition

In any campaign regardless of how well the battalion's organisation works, there will be a gradual reduction in numbers unless there can be replacements and this could not happen for the KOYLI in Burma. The few additions to the infantry involved were of whole battalions such as the Inniskillings airlifted in platoon by platoon in aircraft which took out an equally limited number of refugees. And there were the few who returned to the Battalion from Maymyo after recuperation from wounds or illness. There could be no reinforcements from any previously untapped pool of men who had not been involved in the original mobilisation because they had been away on courses, as sometimes happened elsewhere. Even Wingate's training exercises could not evoke real fear and could only concentrate on physical endurance. In the subsequent victorious advance into Burma a battalion could expect regular periods in reserve, but not in 1942, when disaster piled upon disaster.

Missing in Action?

Fitzpatrick states that 59 men deserted in four hours from Yenangyaung. This is a remarkably exact statement when no records appear to have survived to support it. Surely something as striking as this would have been common knowledge and Ralph Tanner would have heard of it; but there is nothing of this in his diary and the Battalion was already so reduced in numbers that there would have been no hiding such disastrous and demoralising information. At the platoon level social intimacy begins, but it is at the section level that cohesion becomes overwhelmingly important. As the infantry section in which the soldier feels at home is disrupted by the inevitabilities of war, then its members suffer the military equivalent of divorce, desertion, and of course bereavement. In an advance, casualties can be replaced and new faces absorbed into the existing intimate social structure so well described by Fraser, even the sharing of the dead man's kit is part of the process. In a retreat, men from one shattered section are added to another broken up group. In fact, as this Battalion shrunk, the only sense of identity remaining would have been the regiment, a distant construct. Companies shrank and were amalgamated, as were platoons and sections. The sense of rootlessness was scarcely balanced by a vague sense of regimental unity. It was more or less inevitable that some soldiers would get lost, or become merged with the disorganised tail of an army that no longer had any legitimate function or purpose other than survival. The same situation arose in Crete, horrifyingly so in Malaya and Singapore, and no doubt occurred in the flight back into Egypt from Germany's successful attacks in Libya.

The roads back would have been filled with men from base depots who no longer had any purpose: field cashiers, engineering store-men, and hospital staff, for example. It would not be difficult for men to 'disappear' in this crowd, particularly when they were without orders and indeed officers who could give them orders. For a British soldier in Asia, desertion and disappearance into the civilian population was not an option, as it was elsewhere.

What facts are available? The existing records contain an old alphabetical deserters' register in which all the known men in the battalion are listed. This list contains a large number of names listed as missing and as mentioned earlier for 35 men against the word 'missing' is the word 'located', which means that once the battalion had started to reform in Shillong, Assam, they had re-emerged, probably from hospitals and staging camps. This is the total of men who 'disappeared' over five months and we do not know any of the circumstances. Some could easily have been told to go sick, as Ralph Tanner was at Tamu on the Indian border at the end of the march out, but he would be hard put to prove this, except that he spent over three months in hospital and was ultimately invalided home. He cannot even put a date to that. There were no prosecutions for desertion and certainly no suggestion that the persistent drop in the battalion's strength was due to anything more than the attrition of any losing campaign.

Has the contemporary theory of Post Traumatic Stress Disorder any contribution to make to the understanding of what these men endured? Only one officer and one other rank were in the Battalion for the full five months, from start to finish. Most would have experienced warfare at its direst for an average of two to three months, without the periods of relief available in other theatres. Would such continuous stress have dfferent psychological effects than a single experience? Most of the data for this newly identified syndrome is based on single traumatic events involving deaths and disasters. Firemen, policemen and the members of medical response teams of course witness disturbing events, but 40% of identified cases in the UK are soldiers who have experienced combat. The symptoms are listed as recurrent and intrusive recollections, feelings of guilt at having survived, emotional numbness, sleep problems, hyper-vigilance, increased irritability, low self-esteem and significantly impaired memory. We cannot know it, but it would seem likely that most of those who survived this campaign would have had some of these symptoms. Some would have avoided stimuli associated with the campaign such as regimental reunions or social contact with other veterans.

It has been established that parachutists are able to inhibit fear by the frequency of their jumps (Baddeley 1972), but this is continual, not continuous, fear. For the Battalion the possibility of death was a constant and there was nothing that they could do about it except soldier on with their unit, or give up.

Chapter 5

The Other Enemies

Malnutrition

Officer cadets under training at Sandhurst on a daily diet of five thousand calories per day still lose weight. This Battalion, from the time they mobilised and moved to the east side of the Southern Shan States in December 1941 until reaching India would have had a diet consistently below the level adequate to support an active life under field conditions. The diet steadily reduced in both quantity and quality, except for the unexpected beef meals at Indaw and the ration of bottled beer received on the road before Yenangyaung. For some there may have been the occasional addition carried personally, such as the tin of condensed milk Ralph Tanner picked up from a food dump, and from the cases of food left by the Royal Indian Army Service Corps on the side of the road near Yeu to be picked up by men as they passed on their way to Kalewa. From the time of the losses of equipment after the Sittang battle, no soldier would have been carrying a backpack, so all that they had would have been in small sidepacks, if they even had those.

Dehydration

As the retreat continued, the Battalion moved north from the damp lushness of lower Burma into the dry zone of central Burma, and the temperature rose. While the tank men of the 7th Armoured Brigade, around whom the whole retreat pivoted, must have been suffering sitting in their iron boxes, the outsides of which were too hot to touch, this was comfortable in comparison to the lot of the marching infantry. The fact that the enormous Irrawaddy and Chindwin rivers were always to their west and maybe on occasions a few hundred yards away, meant nothing to marching men, that water might just as well have been on the moon. In the later stages some men did not even have water bottles. Near Taungtha the Battalion had to keep marching during the day. The headquarters and escort kept to the track, with its dust stirred up by those in front, but the others had to keep a hundred yards out on either side, marching over rough ground to prevent ambush by the faster marching Japanese and dissident Burmese. These were appalling conditions.

The only occasion which the men had easy access to water was during the river crossings. Walking through the Pin Chaung north of Yenangyaung, where some knelt gratefully to drink after two almost waterless days; being ferried across the Irrawaddy by motor boats manned by Royal Marines; and rowing across the Chindwin in tree trunk canoes. While in later campaigns soldiers were amply provided with water purifying tablets which they could put into their water bottles and drink after a few minutes of shaking, the need for water in this retreat was so great that they would drink anything quickly; the diarrhoea and dysentery that affected almost everyone came from drinking polluted water. For many, the shortage of water was the worst aspect of the retreat, worse than the pursuing enemy. As the Battalion moved north, water became more of a problem as many villages got their water from wells, but they no longer had their buckets and ropes and the infantrymen did not have any. It was much the same in Crete, with water available but agonisingly out of reach in wells.

Dark thoughts and false optimism

The state of mind of these soldiers must have been a factor in whether they survived or not. There was a difference between those who had loved ones in Burma and those who had only themselves to worry about. The former could only hope that the Battalion headquarters in Maymyo had got their women and children out of danger. Both groups would have been uplifted by getting mail but none came in after Yenangyaung. Ralph Tanner received no mail for five months and nothing that he sent home arrived. A postcard from his mother circulated amongst numerous addresses in India before eventually being returned to her, so that as far as his family were concerned he was 'missing'.

Most men would have felt themselves increasingly alone as companies became platoons and platoons sections. They were skittles being knocked over by forces over which neither they nor their superiors had control. Nevertheless, personal hopes that things were going to get better probably dominated – they usually do, even in the most extreme difficulties. Major Throckmorton in his post-campaign description of events wrote on 29 April, 'To our great joy the news arrived that our brigade was to move to Monywa, embark on a steamer and sail up the Chindwin to Kalewa.' The Japanese got to Monywa first. During the march north of Pyingaing the Colonel said that there was a possibility of getting transport from Pantha oilfield onwards; the possibility became a probability, then in the minds of many a certainty; but there were no lorries there, nor ever had been.

Illness

The dividing line between clinical illness and psychosomatic distress is not always clear and indeed quite impossible to determine under field conditions. In the initial stages of the campaign it was possible to be marked down as ill because of a high temperature and persistent diarrhoea and sent back to the base hospital to recover. At the end, there were 126 men in the Alexandra barracks in Maymyo who had been defined by some medical authority as ill and who eventually reached India under the base commander Captain Fox, who had earlier been partially incapacitated by an attack of poliomyelitis. As the campaign continued the number of men who contracted dysentery and malaria inexorably rose as preventive measures were non-existent. After five months all the men still with the battalion were probably clinically ill. In the final stages, a man with an attack of malaria would continue to march, as the alternative would be to drop out and in effect be left to die. Even if there was a medical officer there in the later stages, any diagnosis he could make would be academic. If we assume an original strength for the Battalion of under 550, of which 122 are known to have died, and about 70 men were with the battalion at the Indian border, the 126 men in the depot is not an unexpected figure for drop-outs from illness, given the conditions under which they had been living.

Assumed Battalion Strength	550
Killed	122
Ill at Depot	126
Missing/Unaccounted for	232
Number entering India	70

The known dead are outnumbered by the missing. The unofficial casualty list gives 109 as missing with a date, sometimes with a range of possible dates within which they died. Even this has mistakes in it, as one man listed on the war memorial as dead was in fact a survivor.

Lost to the forest

All the Battalion records were lost when the depot in Alexandria Barracks in Maymyo was evacuated by Capt Fox in March. The buildings were first looted by the Burmese and then occupied by the Japanese in April. When the Battalion came to be reconstituted in Shillong, some attempt was made to record details. Records did exist but they are now lost. Captain Fox, for example, wrote to Ralph Tanner later about the money he had paid out to Burmese for shooting the cow near Indaw and he was repaid (see Diary reference in Appendix A).[11]

None of the men listed as dead on the Rangoon cemetery war memorial have a known grave. Some indeed were buried, like Major Martin who died of his burns. Ralph was told that he had been buried on the northern edge of Kalewa village on the Chindwin and although he passed on this information to the post-war Grave Recovery Unit, which tried to bring all bodies into the one Commonwealth War Cemetery near to Rangoon, it was never found. One must assume that those known to have been killed in action or died of their wounds and recorded as such in the published Battalion history were left lying where they died. There does not seem to be any record from the Japanese side of burying or burning British and Indian dead. They may well have done so, particularly as General Sakurai commanding 33 Division put up a monument at Yenangyaung soon after the campaign was over to the British and Indian dead as well as to the Japanese casualties.

Explosions, sudden dispersals because of aircraft attacks and accidents would have dispersed even small groups of men well known to each other and in the hurricane of war, looking for someone is not a priority. In the conditions of Burma in 1942 it is unlikely that any officer would have kept records and even if he did none has survived. Major Martin took the identity disc off the driver of the lorry hit by a shell on the Taungdwingyi-Magwe road but as he himself died from burns a month later; that man, whoever he was, from an unknown unit, remains unidentified. Even if his next of kin had made enquiries as to what had happened to him, no one would have been able to say more than that on one date he was there and on another date he was not.

Before he joined the Battalion in Yenangyaung in early March on Intelligence work Ralph Tanner found two KOYLI privates in a small township hospital south of Magwe. A doctor told him that they were there and he did not know what to do with them. Ralph suspected that one had a self-inflicted wound and the other had stayed with him. He had no idea how they got there in the first place but he advised them to get out and go north as quickly as possible. Ralph does not know what happened to them; perhaps they were listed as missing and then maybe marked as located later somewhere in India. Colonel Bernard Fergusson used the phrase 'lost to the forest' in his book *The Wild Green Earth* about the first Wingate incursion into Japanese-occupied Burma, referring to men who had just disappeared. These men were not seen to collapse, were not seen to have been killed or left behind as wounded or sick and unable to walk anymore. It had been explained to participants during training that once they crossed the Chindwin river, it was inevitable that they marched or they died. This is why 'missing' in the reconstructed roll of the Battalion is the commonest classification for those who were not known to have survived. At one hourly halt between Pyingaing and Pantha, one man disappeared. It was only a ten-minute halt and the column could not have stayed to look for him since they were moving in order of battalions in the brigade. What happened to him?

He could not have deserted in the middle of an uninhabited forest, there were no Japanese about and it seems unlikely that there were Burmese lurking in the hope of picking up abandoned property. It may be that he got lost when going off on his own to excrete or just collapsed and died. General Wingate advised those with dysentery just to excrete as they walked and clean themselves up later, as the effort required to squat down, excrete and then to catch up was an enormous expenditure of energy. Whatever happened, this man was indeed lost to the forest.

Part of the tragedy is that so many men died not in some thunderous, historically well known battleground, about which their relatives would have known. These KOYLI men died in unknown and unknowable circumstances, perhaps unnecessarily. Taffy Philipps, the efficient and much respected Quartermaster who had done so much to keep the Battalion going, died of exhaustion on the Pin Chaung. Forty years later his son-in-law wrote to Ralph asking about the circumstances of his death, about which his family had heard nothing.[12]

The failure of communications

The primary, insoluble problem for command and control during the retreat was the isolation of units. While early on there was some line communication between battalion headquarters and companies, this soon came to an end as there were no replacements for lost handsets and wire. Right from the start, the Battalion had not been provided with wireless sets and it had no trained wireless operators or people proficient in Morse code. Throughout World War II wireless sets were available but they were heavy and their range was correlated to their size. They were dependent on fragile valves and heavy batteries that constantly needed recharging.

They were too heavy for an individual soldier to carry far and thus depended on motor transport, carts, or pack mules. So wireless communication was never an option. Later in the campaign when the remnants of I Bur Brigade were moving across country north of Pyingaing the Brigade had one such cumbersome wireless set with its trained operator but it could only receive messages. So communication between brigade and battalion and battalion to companies was by personal messengers. The only unit which was in overall wireless communication with its members must have been the 7th Armoured Brigade, in which each tank had its wireless set. It is probable that the tanks on occasions carried messages to other units. The carrying of messages by individual messengers across country possibly occupied by intrusive Japanese patrols or their advancing columns and which might also have contained hostile Burmese, was always going to be a hazardous undertaking. It required courage, stamina and initiative; but at least on foot, the messenger would have not have been as visible or audible as he would be on motorcycle or horseback. In early March, Ralph overheard a senior staff officer near Taungdwingyi saying that he should have twenty despatch riders available for the necessary flow of orders but that he only had four. One part of the Thockmorton report states: 'This was the third time in five days that orders had failed to reach the Battalion.' The worst of these failures was the order to withdraw from Migyaungyee, carried by 2/Lieut. Watts, riding a horse possibly for the first time from which he was thrown and injured, so the message was never received.

For much of the campaign the CO of the Battalion was blind, dependent on personally carried messages and on his own interpretation of events. Except for the 7th Armoured Brigade, it is not too far fetched to suggest that the methods of communication were not much of an improvement on those of the Crimea and the Indian Mutiny of the mid 1800s.

The civilian population

In the thunder and crash of close order warfare the attitude of the local population is irrelevant, if indeed they stayed in the area. But in mobile fighting in which units rarely stay more than a few days in one place, the attitude of civilians as suppliers of information to both sides is of great importance. The local Burmese certainly did not supply the Battalion with any information about Japanese movements because they did not stay around to talk and only the two locally recruited Anglo-Burmans knew enough Burmese to carry on a conversation. The locals would have known that their interests lay in keeping out of the way and that there was no advantage in helping what was obviously the losing side – and the soldiers of a colonial government. This did not mean that they were actively hostile, but the indigenous population would have heard about, if not read, Japanese nationalist propaganda. It is understandable that villagers provided the Japanese with information as to where the British-Indian forces were temporarily settled and how to outflank them. Pat Carmichael in his book *Mountain Battery* (1983) baldly stated: 'I think we loathed the Burmans almost as much as we did the Japanese, for their persistent treachery and murderous attacks on refugees.'

There was also the actively hostile Burmese minority with officers under Aung San trained by the Japanese Army and with Japanese officers attached to them on the line of retreat from Prome to Yenangyaung, who ambushed the Battalion sporadically. The Battalion was always surrounded by a spider's web of passive hostility. The shooting of so many supposed looters at Taungtha would certainly have persuaded no Burmese that it would be in their interests to approach either British or Indian soldiers. It should be remembered that it had been Indian soldiers who had conquered Burma for the British and had enforced the regime since. The large majority of Rangoon's population were Tamils from southern India.

However, as the Battalion moved north into the mountains, this resentment was replaced by active support. The population there was administered under a different system of government; the Burma Frontier Service tacitly supported the people's historical hostility to the lowland Burmese. The British had endeavoured to protect the hill tribes – the Shans, the (largely Christian) Karens and others – from exploitation by their lowland cousins. The Battalion ended up in an area which the Japanese, had they followed up their advance, would have found far less sympathetic to their demands.

In discussing the civilian population, there is a danger that the terrible suffering of the refugees is forgotten. Those Indians fleeing before the Japanese were of course civilians and many were born in Burma. Most of those who escaped followed the same route as the bulk of the Burma Army, joining somewhere along the line Kalewa, Tamu, Palel, Imphal. There were other routes, even more arduous. Estimates as to deaths on the journey vary incredibly widely, from 10,000 to 120,000. Something like half a million Indians succeeded in escaping from Burma.

1 Meeting in Tokyo, 1985; 2/Lieut. R. Tanner discussing the action at Toksan, as guest of four officers from the Japanese 33 Division.

2 The Whole battalion on parade, 1937; KOYLI publicity brochure of life at Alexandra Barracks Maymyo.

3 KOYLI officers.

4 Ceremonial march through Maymyo.

5 The Regimental Colours, 1936, Minden Day.

6 'B' Company with their trophies, 1936.

7 The Ladies Club outside the Sergeants Mess.

8 & *9* Leave camp activities circa 1936.

10 & *11* From the 2/KOYLI publicity brochure, leave camp.

12 Officers south of Yenangyaung, 16 April; Major D. Martin, Lt.-Col. Chadwick and Major Throckmorton during a ten-minute halt.

13 2/KOYLI crossing the Pin Chaung north of Yenangyaung, 19 April.

14 Officers at Kantha, 16 April; Major D. Martin and Major Wardleworth during the halt at Kantha.

15 Officers at Taungtha, 25 April; Chinese Captain, 2/Lieuts. Tanner and Marsh and the Corporal who died of burns.

16 Officers at Mount Popa, 20 April; left to right: Lieut. Fitzpatrick, Capt. Baxter, Lt. Col. Chadwick, 2/Lieut. Tanner, Major Wardleworth, Major Martin.

17 Lt.-Col. Chadwick collecting firewood at Pyingaing, 7 May.

18 A ten-minute halt between Pawlaw and Chinyaung, 9 May.

19 Ten-minute halt between Pantha and Chintaung, 9 May.

20 River crossing between Lawtha and Pantha, 12 May.

21 Lieut. Stephenson, a survivor with multiple jungle sores, at Dehra Dun General Hospital, early June 1942.

22 Mitsubishi Ki-51 officially designated the Army Type 99 Assault Plane, code-named 'Sonia' by the Allies.

23 The bridge over the Sittang.

24 A famous picture of the Japanese approaching the Yenangyaung oilfields.

Chapter 6

Conclusions

The re-establishment of the Battalion

As we have seen, when the Battalion reached Tamu on the India-Burma border there were only some seventy men out of some five hundred still standing. Add to these the 126 sick and two officers at Alexandra barracks in the hill town of Maymyo, north-east of Mandalay. Under Captain Fox the latter reached India independently, burying the regimental silver en route but retaining the regimental colours. 117 men and six officers are recorded as missing or killed and a further thirty men died as prisoners of war or in hospital in India.

There is no record of this in the regimental history, but Ralph Tanner was advised by the officer concerned that one company of the 2/KOYLI had been put on the west bank of the Irrawaddy river to confront the Japanese. They marched north to India without ever encountering any enemy. They also would have been part of the recovery of the Battalion in Shillong, to which were added reinforcements from Britain.

The Battalion began to be reconstituted in the pleasant surroundings of the Assamese hill station of Shillong around the core of survivors, together with a number who 'drifted in' from various depots and hospitals in India. It then acted as an internal security force for two years and was not included in any fighting formation until it became part of the preparations for the invasion of Malaya, which did not take place because of the Japanese surrender.

The lessons of war

These men retained a sense of cohesion and maintained a belief in the possibility of survival through continual disasters. The attrition rate looks appalling but it is thrown into stark relief by the fact that the Battalion started with a fixed number of men and received no reinforcements, except for a number of newly commissioned officers. The losses might well have been no different had the Battalion been going the other way into Burma later in the War, except for casualties from malaria and malnutrition. At the end of five months following a battalion's entry into Western Europe after D-Day, for example, there was usually about 20% of the original strength still serving. About 10% of KOYLI reached Imphal at the end of the campaign but there were over a hundred who were at the Maymyo depot who also got out.

Optimistic rumour was a constant subject for these soldiers and had the peculiar feature of not being all that disturbing when it proved to be untrue. High flying Japanese bombers were taken to be the RAF going to 'bash the Japs', and the hope of transport at Indaw helped men to march, even when the transport turned out to be one burnt-out lorry. This rumour mill is part of the parallel, informal life of an institution, which helps the overall system to work.

The regimental spirit did not allow blame for their predicament to be placed within the regimental framework, nor indeed with the army in Burma. Considering the length of the retreat and the absence of any possible outside help, except for the timely intervention of the Chinese at Yenangyaung, the standard of support staff work was of a high quality when there was so little to go around.

The Japanese moved cross-country at speed and the British-Indian army stuck to roads, but it was only the availability of transport that allowed so many to get to India. In these circumstances the Battalion marched well enough under appalling conditions.

Training did not push men into the conditions they were likely to experience in the field and manoeuvres were sham. Learning the local language was simply not on the agenda; it is likely that except for local recruits no one in the Battalion was able to say please and thank you in Burmese.

Extraordinary acts of bravery and initiative should be recognised more, such as the bravery of Corporal Hart to whom this study is dedicated, and Major Wardleworth in swimming the Chindwin. A Colonel's note to this effect in Part Two orders should be a matter of regimental record.

Many of the disasters which these men suffered were the result of messages not getting through and were not the result of human failings. Much that happened to these men could have been even worse, had it not been for their personal ability to recover and the quality of the senior officers with which they started and continued to have in the terrible retreat. Cede nullis.[13]

Appendix A

The Diary of 2/Lieut. R. Tanner, 223473

This diary was compiled in 1943 from notes and detailed maps of the retreat which Ralph Tanner carried back from the conflict. All additional editorial comments are shown in the footnotes. There have been no changes to spelling, grammar or punctuation unless indicated [ ]. Comments regarding apparently missing or unreadable words are shown in the same way. He has presented the diary as it was written and added comments in the first person in the 1970s and in 2006. These comments are shown separately from the diary text. There will perforce be duplications and inconsistencies.

Before it was typed the diary was in three different styles of Ralph Tanner's handwriting: a pencil scrawl under some dates, some notes pinned to dates written on sheets of US army message pads which he had acquired in Myitkyina, north Burma, where he had been sent with a lorry to pick up anything he could get hold of as the US army there was pulling out, and many pages of cramped handwriting forming the bulk of the diary, written in a British government notebook.

The date for the final entries cannot have been earlier than October 1945, when he got the US message pads. The majority was written in 1944 when he was a captain in MI2d, in the War Office, London. There he was able to get maps of Burma and to read the situation reports from Burma and India, which were the same ones on which Lt-Col Chadwick based his reconstructed War Diary.

On joining in Egypt an ex-commando contingent for Mission 204 based in north Burma and destined to go into China as a guerrilla support group, I was Private 6970623. We embarked at Calcutta in the dark and sailed to Rangoon in the ship, which had hundreds of Indian labourers travelling on the deck to work there; I was told it was an annual migration.

We stayed in the Gloucester Regiment's barracks outside Rangoon of which I remember nothing except disliking travelling by rickshaw, which I did not ever do again. Humans should not be pulled about by other humans as beasts of burden. In this and other places there was never much incentive for other ranks to leave the barracks and go into town; there was nowhere much to go, they did not know the language and it was expensive since we were then on the equivalent of 7 shillings per week. There was always a canteen in the barracks. In Maymyo the Salvation Army ran a place where you could get egg and chips so I suspect the only reason for going out of barracks was to find a woman, since there were no regimental brothels with approved and inspected women. I remember prophylactic centres in Cairo for trying to deal with the after effects but I do not think the same existed in Burma. We were told that it was a military offence to get VD, which could be used to evade war duty. On the ship out it was also regarded as a military offence to get so sunburnt as to be unable to perform duty.

We then travelled by train to Mandalay. On the platform there, Indian policemen were guarding a bunch of Burmese prisoners who were chained together. The train up to Maymyo went backward and forwards up the escarpment. There was a sense of excitement for me, as if we were going into the unknown. I was disappointed in Maymyo when I saw horse-drawn carriages outside the station.

The unit which we joined was called Military Mission 204 but for political reasons it was called the Bush Warfare School. It included an Australian platoon. The machine gun on which we trained was the one in use in the Chinese army; it was not the Bren. I understood it to be Czech; it had a square, not a curved magazine. The camp was in newly-built wooden and thatched buildings to the north of Maymyo. At the end of the War when I was in M12d in the War office I looked at air photos and there was no trace of the whole camp. In the buildings the beds were straw mattresses on a raised platform running down the length of the building with a large square box for our kit. Each of us employed a local lad to clean our boots and equipment. A barber toured these barrack rooms before reveille and shaved you in bed with a cut throat razor, often without even waking you up, for a rupee a week. Another man circulated a box of books, you bought one and then sold it back to him. It was an easy life in an ideal climate at about three thousand feet.

It was three months more or less before the Jap war broke out. Certain exercises stick in my mind. Learning to use anti-tank stick-on grenades in a glass bubble which had to be thrown at a tank; there was one premature burst but I had already turned my back. Then sinking oil drums in an embankment, which could be made to explode sideways on to passing vehicles. One pound of gun cotton will cut an inch of steel like a railway line. The gelignite, if kept in one position in a box, leaked into one part of the stick and became unreliable. Handling gelignite, because of its tackiness, gave one a bad headache, which I got. I also seem to remember that we were told that bridges had to be blown up unevenly or they just settled back and another rough bridge could be built on top of them.

Major Calvert Royal Engineers was on the staff and he later became a Brigadier General in the Chindits. He used to put time pencil detonators in the walls of the HQ to see how reliable their timing was. I remember nothing more about him.

We had one night out after a route march and camped near a Shan village. I remember the wooden buildings and the Shan headman in his turban coming out of the dark. Robinson also wanted to find out how far a group could march in 24 hours. I think they managed 56 miles.[14] I remember little of this man, except I think he was the son of a jeweller from Chelmsford. I learnt that you ironed kilts from the inside through brown paper. He was no more Scottish that I was.

We went by lorry up to Lashio and stayed in barracks there and I remember reading Olaf Stapledon's Pelican on philosophy sitting on the steps of the barracks. Robinson took us all to a Chinese meal in which there were many dishes. Either going or coming we stopped near a hill side with a wonderful view. The Gohteik gorge was impressive with its zigzag road on the north side, up which a convey of lorries was crawling towards China; I think they were all three-tonners so not much can have been carried to Kunming.

Out of my 14 (?) rupees per week pay and the extra which I got as a soldier servant I think I did quite well. I bought a camera and a watch.[15] I also bought a 22 magazine rifle but I have no idea from whom or under what deal but it went off once in the barrack room as I had left it loaded, I must have pulled the trigger. It nearly hit someone. A salutary lesson. If you pulled the magazine backwards and forwards while the trigger was pressed, it acted as an automatic.

At Maymyo there was range practice and I fired a machine gun from the hip at metal plates. It was easy to correct the direction of the fire with each burst. I also had a dog because I suppose I was in need of something to lavish affection on. Someone else had a monkey and another a puppy and they were both made drunk on beer. I went for a walk in the hills behind the camp and recall being excited by the sight of a Scarlet Minivet in the trees.

At one time I had a poisoned hand and went into the military hospital for a day or two where it was cut open etc. I was already developing the periodic diarrhoea from amoebic dysentery which I may have caught in Egypt but which I never did anything about because it never seemed bad enough to go off duty. I do not remember that the start of the Jap war was a noticeable occasion but I do remember being in the canteen when it came through that the *Prince of Wales* had been sunk.

There was a rumour that I had got the MM for Crete, which must have been something to do with being Mentioned in despatches in December, but I never knew about this until much later when a master from school who kept these sort of records wrote to my parents to enquire whether Private R. Tanner was the boy who had been in his class at Rugby. In fact I never remember being informed about this until at the end of the War I got the official printed citation. Sometime someone must have suggested that I apply for a commission but I cannot remember having filled in any form. I remember an interview with a colonel on the station staff and that's all. I did not go on any training course. On a Friday I was Private 6970623 and on Monday I was 2/Lt 223473 in the 2nd battalion of the KOYLI whose HQ was in Maymyo, but the Battalion was away fighting in the south of Burma.

So suddenly I was an officer. I had no money to buy a uniform so I was lent 100 rupees by an officer in the Bush Warfare School called Handley-Derry who had worked in the Hong Kong and Shanghai bank in Shanghai; many years later I tried to find out through that bank in London whether he was still alive so that I could repay him but I never got a reply. I moved into a house in the cantonment which was already occupied by the Army pathologist who was profoundly deaf and so had taken up this specialisation because he could not function as a doctor, and a dubious character called Bruce, an American who had been in the Shanghai police who wandered around armed with a revolver. I had an Indian servant. The pathologist thought I had amoebic dysentery from the smell; I came across him later from seeing a letter by him in the British Medical Journal and he was then farming in Bourton Far Hill farm above Moreton-in-Marsh.

The depot commander was a Captain Fox who was not fit enough from an attack of polio to serve in the field. As a territorial in the Artists Rifles he knew my brother. I remember having to post the evening guard from what I could remember of guard mounting when I was in the depot of the Royal Berkshire Regiment in Reading. I did not know that the KOYLI was a light infantry regiment and started all their drill movements from the 'at ease' position.

The men in the depot had been invalided from the front or were too out of condition to go in the first place. I went to some sort of party and was politely ticked off by the wife of the RSM for referring to the regiment as the Koylies rather than KOYLI. A rather beautiful young woman recently married to Major Wardleworth was there but she was killed soon after by bombing on Myitkyina airfield when she was about to be evacuated by air. I bought a wireless from a nurse/wife/daughter who was being evacuated and felt proud of owning such a piece of property.

I read some reports. Little Jap equipment had been captured and it seemed to have been of a rather simple quality. Another was from a senior medical officer noting the high number of malaria casualties and that men were not sleeping under their mosquito nets in the field. I thought then from my field experience in Crete, how in the hell were men in action supposed to put up mosquito nets and maybe get trapped inside them if there was an alarm? I think I ate in the mess on some occasions but there were very few officers on the station and I cannot remember who they were or even if I talked to them, or they to me. As I could not drive and it now seemed very necessary, I was taught to drive by a sergeant in Captain Fox's Ford which had double declutching. We just went out on the road and I started to drive. I cannot remember more than a couple of lessons before I could manage the vehicle.

March 8

Set out from Maymyo early morning

I was given the job of escorting the Battalion's wives down to Magwe airfield where they were to be evacuated by air. These included British wives of soldiers who had come to Burma with the Battalion and the wives who had been married locally and they were all living in the Battalion's married quarters. One was a large Hindu woman and another a young Burmese girl whom I remember breast feeding her baby on the roadside at Yenangyaung.

Before I left I put all my possessions in the large attaché case which I had brought from Egypt and left it in the regimental store. Obviously I never saw that again but after the War I did see a Tootal tie with red spots in a shop in Lashio, which I thought had been mine. I did not bother to buy it.

The wives were all transported in perhaps two three-ton lorries with the one attaché case each they were allowed. I think we stayed one night in Mandalay and then one night in Yenangyaung where the wives of the oil company employees looked after them for the night. Next morning I took them to Magwe and they were all packed into a B17 with an American crew. One of the crew said to me that they wanted some damn bombs and did not like doing this sort of job. All these women had now lost all their private possessions and did not in fact know whether their husbands were still alive or not. I do not think that any showed any emotion; they were perhaps too stunned as well as having lost all their possessions. These same aircraft brought in a battalion of the Inniskillings and I spent the night in their camp in the open near Magwe, from whom I borrowed a blanket. I think this was their first active service role. [There was an American War Correspondent with them (Belden 1943).]

After this I was somehow attached to an oil company man called Higginbotham, a Burmese speaker, to set up some sort of an intelligence network as the Japanese advanced. I do not know why this was so but I visited a number of sub-police stations and talked to the sub-inspectors about what they had to watch out for and report. I photographed some. I had exchanged my fold-out camera for a much smaller one taking 120 film and I carried this through to India; if not, how else would I still have these photographs?

I had no idea of the rapidity of the campaign or that we were losing ground fast. There was very little on the shelves of the Army Indian store in Yenangyaung except bottles of liquor and he remarked that nothing was coming through. So presumably then Rangoon had not yet been evacuated.

I visited Taungdwingyi and stayed with the Burmese Superintendent of Police who told me that the coocal bird was inedible but it was called the subaltern's pheasant, as it was so often shot by newcomers. He and his assistant asked for arms. I also visited places north of Taungdwingyi where there was a railway line which I think that Indian engineers were starting to pull up so that the track could be used as a road. I remember one PWD inspector who came from the Arakan who implored me to find him a rifle but I had none to give. But this may have been later.

I was then driving an America saloon car. On the Kyaukpadaung road to Meiktial I went round an army lorry and nearly knocked down a driver who was standing beside it. I think that I was not yet fully in control of a car. I seem to remember that I did not understand that when you put the brake on, you let out the clutch. At one place on the main road south where I stopped the doctor said that he had two soldiers in the hospital. I visited them as they were worried what was going to happen to them as they had gunshot wounds in the legs (?). I said that they should get out and move north as fast as they could. I had the impression that these were self-inflicted wounds and that they were KOYLI but I have no idea how they had got there.

I visited the Deputy Commissioner at Magwe, who was pessimistic that any of the sub-inspectors, particularly one, would ever act as agents. I wanted to see if I could have any leave and enquired of him whether there was a forest rest house which I could go to for a few days. I was deluded that this might even be possible but I had had no leave since the end of Crete, the previous June. Then the Battalion turned up at Yenangyaung and I went to them, as Higginbotham was getting ready to evacuate himself. I slept the last night at his house in a bed on the lawn to get away from the heat of the house (I presume that by then the electricity generator might have been blown). He had a pair of Churchill shotguns which he was going to take with him.

I can remember no documentation at all about being commissioned except that Fox at the depot gave me a self-composed identity card with a photograph and the depot stamp. But I was being paid because after the campaign my account had been transferred from Rangoon to Amritsar. As far as I recollect my account had been so-many rupees when I saw it last and when it had got to Amritsar it had doubled. So presumably money had been paid in after I had left the depot. I cashed at least one cheque with a Field Cashier and these were all lost during the campaign so I was never debited their sums, indeed I had no idea what I had cashed, when and where. Any orders that I received after I had left the depot were verbal ones, (indeed, the instructions for the family evacuation were not written). But other than a field security corporal in Imphal who asked me to identify myself, and I had the depot identity card, no one ever questioned who I was.

The remains of the Battalion had been pulled back into reserve for a rest. I was attached to headquarters, the Adjutant was Major David Martin. His father was in Singapore and I think his mother was Maltese. He had a conch shell tattooed on this left shoulder.

We shared a bedroom in one of the Burma Oil Company houses. One afternoon when we were having a siesta, we heard bombing to the south. It was the destruction of the remaining RAF on Magwe airfield as well as the Flying Tigers.

I was provided with a soldier servant with whom presumably I travelled. I cannot remember his name (but the nominal roll named him as Hood). Before I joined the Battalion I cannot remember what my duties were, but I must have been told to do something to the south because I visited Magwe airfield, which was totally deserted with damaged, but seemingly entire aeroplanes littering the tarmac. There were Blenheims and the P40 of the Flying Tigers with shark noses painted on the cowling. I took some photographs but as they were against the light they came out badly.

I went to the RAF barracks on the slopes some way from the airfield and they seemed to have left in a hurry with clothes all over the place and no sign that the Burmese had come in to loot. I picked up a pair of fur-lined flying boots. There were no signs that these buildings had been machine-gunned from the air, although they were very conspicuous on a bare slope.

I think it was in this period that I visited the villages to the east and north of Taungdwingyi for which I had borrowed a jeep. The road was very rough and I broke both front springs of the vehicle. I started to try and cook the rice which I had with me but found that I did not know how to do it.

One day we were visited by General Alexander and I saw him talking to Lt Col Chadwick from an upstairs window. The battalion IO was very worried because he had found broken glass on the road between the European houses and the local village, Twingone.

Somewhere we spent the night near to a flowing stream, possibly the Pinchaung, and I noticed the Engineers' flags that marked off the areas to be used for human, then animal drinking, for bathing and then cleaning clothes. There were Sikhs there and I remember a pair wandering about in the striped underpants holding hands. (Then the war proper caught up).

March 9

Night at Meiktila Burf lines 9/10

March 10
Spent 10/11 night in Yenangyaung club in little room off entrance[16]

March 11
Night 11/12 at Innisks camp
Saw evacuees off at aerodrome in morning[17]
Started from Yenangyaung

March 12
While at Magwe Adv. Burma army passed Innisks camp on way North
Night 12/13 Innisks camp

March 13
Yenangyaung

March 14–29 [no entries]

March 21
Magwe heavily bombed in afternoon

March 22
Magwe heavily bombed 0930hrs and 13.30hrs
Still at Yenangyaung
In bath at Yenangyaung at time of first bombing[18]

March 27–March 30 [no entries]

March 31
On "I" [intelligence] work in Taungdwingyi area

Magwe bombed in afternoon twice by six bombers and sixteen aircraft machine-gunning

I was in the town at the almost derelict RAF headquarters overlooking the grass green [polo ground] in the centre of the town near the jail, after bombing of which I heard there was no sound of machine gunning and they came over my head in formations of three. I cannot remember what they looked like except I thought the bombers were single engined jobs and flying lower than fighters. The HAA [Heavy Anti-Aircraft] battery stationed on the rising ground on the Taunggyi road just as it branches to the left for the short cut round the town coming out by the aerodrome, opened fire but there appeared to be no close ones and the planes remained in formation at 2000 feet+ going down the line of the river to the South. I was passing through on my way to Taungdwingyi

Magwe bombing

While on intelligence work, passing through at about 3 in afternoon. I was in central place near polo ground. AA battery stationed a little to the east of the road junction for detour round Magwe. As far as remembered single engined light bombers going and coming over centre of town, in formation, about twelve; took no evasive action. At no more than 2000 feet. Another six fighters circling at 10,000 or more. No bombing in town. Airfield totally deserted.[19]

April 1–April 10 [no entries]

April 11

Set out from YENANGYAUNG Night 11/12 on road to milestone 305

Movement ordered for 1800hrs; RIASC transport companies allocated for the work. Late start; I was in one of the last trucks with Bn headquarters personnel including the lance-corporal who could speak Burmese and orderly room sergeant who had had a parcel sent down from his father-in-law who ran Fosters Hotel in Maymyo and his wife, with food in it. Darkness came very quickly as it was dark when we passed the burning tank farm, although it was a long halt for the convoy to form up on the straight piece of road from the garrison

Bn barracks to the Yenangyaung treasury on the corner by the club. The tank farm was burning furiously with a weird appearance as the clouds of black smoke from the oil cloaked the flames and there was a straightforward contrast between the flames and the smoke with little intermediate glow as with normal fires. Pass long columns of animal transport going south, I think unloaded, both carts and mules.

Bn had been ordered to proceed to MIGYAUNGYE under command of 1BURDIV and Capt Anne (an officer from KOYLI on staff duty) Staff Captain for 1 Bde, met convoy of lorries just before the road branched off to the right for MIGYAUNGYE, he had a conference with Lt-Col CHADWICK, Bn commander and explained to him by hurricane lantern the field sketches he had made of suggested positions in the village; just as they were about to move off, a DR arrived and gave CHADWICK a message to the effect that the Bn was to come under 13 Bde and was to move to milestone [unknown number] and bivouac for the night beside the road and await further orders. Convoy moved onto milestone [unknown number] and debussed, whereupon CHADWICK and DAVID[20] with some others tried to recce in the dark with my torch, it wasn't very successful so the four companies were formed into a square with the trucks enclosed; Bn HQ was under a very large tree. There was no moon; no outside movement could be heard. All headquarters officers did night watch, I was on about 0300hrs, it was chilly, not cold, there was a heavy dew. Guards were posted by companies.

April 12

Road block formed at milestone 305 near SAINGGYA. Night 12/13 at THITYAGAUK

'Stand-to' before first light (general operational rule) nothing happened. Breakfast was made by companies beside lorries in ditches. A message came in during the early morning ordering us to remain here and take up a position covering a road block which we were to make; Bn headquarters was to be in a little village off the roads to the left down a track. A road block was formed with a broken down bullock cart and some wood and stones, and Lieut FITZPATRICK sited his mortars behind some bushes to the north edge of the road. Transport trucks were distributed to coys and dispersed under them. We were also supposed to receive a complete allotment of mules and carts sometime in the morning. I was changed over from Liaison Officer to Transport Officer in anticipation of their arrival. Message came through that there was enemy movement across our front rough parallel to the TAUNGD-WINGYI road going east. Transport materialised and was dispersed in the village. [Japanese] Recce plane materialised at eight o'clock. Little movement along the road.

April 13

All day at THITYAGAUK; move off in evening. Night beside trucks at TOKSAN

Stand-to in the early morning, no activity. 13 Brigade took no offensive action during the morning as apparently the enemy could not be located, so the Bn came back from across the road where they were on the southern perimeter. There was a line laid from Bde to Bn. I went to the Bde HQ once during the morning with someone else over the question of animal transport and we looked at the Sitmap propped up on a tree; if I remember rightly the Japs were going north about four miles to the east, having just crossed the TUANGD-WINGYI which had not been cut during the night. Bombers went over once going north.

April 14

Attacked at dawn. Day adrift, rejoin Bn in evening. Night before crossing the Chaung.

On waking at first light, the troops were standing to very poorly and the main body of the Bn was still unlocated, 'Taffy'

Williams who was nominally commanding ordered me to take a guide who was supposed to have helped us last night, and go and find the Bn. Like a fool I only took my fighting equipment, leaving my pack, and started north parallel to the edge of TOKSAN village, we hadn't gone very far (400 yds at most) when there was a solitary shot followed almost immediately by mg bursts and light mortar explosions, all behind us; I immediately accelerated; but after searching vainly for half-an-hour and seeing no one, moved a little to the west up the rise from the river and came upon a pungyi-chaung where we asked for food. The priests or villagers said that the meal wasn't ready but they gave us bananas and water which both of us disposed of very quickly. I was scared they would double-cross us and I kept the other bloke well away from the line of fire of my TSMG[21] which I kept on my arm while I ate, the natives watched us and seemed friendly but I hated to turn my back on them when we walked away; outside their compound was an embankment and we lay on top and watched the countryside; below us about a mile away lay TOKSAN, a file of troops, presumably Japs, was moving into the village from the left, but otherwise there was no sign of movement, firing was going on heavily and bullets kept hitting the dust in front of us. I put my hands to my eyes as if I was holding binoculars to shade my eyes from the sun, I watched for about ten minutes and then a sniper put a bullet through and under my armpit hitting the dust up into my face. I rolled off the embankment quickly swearing so much that the other bloke thought I was hit. We decided to move off after that, down towards the river as I didn't think that the Japs would have [gone] through there yet; we wandered about for some time in that direction and saw nothing except an abandoned British haversack with some TSMG magazines which I pocketed; soon after that we on were a cart track with high hedges when the firing stopped for some time, three Jap single-engined fixed undercarriage planes came over and circled slowly searching the ground;[22]

they did so for ten minutes and apparently seeing nothing flew off; they arrived about one hour after if I remember rightly, certainly not much more after the firing stopped. As the planes had gone and the firing stopped it did not occur to me that the Japs might have won, so I naturally thought that our own force had won the action and the Japs withdrawn. On thinking it all over again I remember that there was a first period of firing, then quite a long pause and then the firing started again and then finally died down with no recurrence. We then moved back towards the village until we were about two to three hundred yards away, when I saw movement, we got down in the hedge and watched; there Japs and Burmese moving our trucks to the edge of the village and unloading them, I actually saw one little bastard on my truck where I had left my haversack with all my precious photos and writings. We watched for a few minutes, when the other man suddenly whispered "flatten yourself" and I got down in the dust; actually we had arranged to stay there for sometime doing twenty-minute watches each, but I had only shut my eyes for five when this happened; there were about four, khaki clad, helping another up a tree on the other side of our field about one hundred yards away. Crawling on our faces we managed to get through the cactus edge and down the other side into a small chaung where we were safe from view and could walk away into the hollow. We rested there for a little while, thinking how lucky we were to be alive; rested there for a few minutes about two hundred yards from the road which we had come down to Toksan as it went onto MYINGUN. I saw someone looking over the cactus hedge from beside the road, I thought he saw me and soon disappeared, I at once started to move towards the river but slightly northwards for about half-a-mile stopping at a grove of light trees. We lay down there again to rest taking a mouthful of water every half hour until after midday; an old Indian appeared soon after a flock of goats had nibbled their way past us, I tried to hit one with my rifle butt so that we could get some milk to drink but I missed, he told us that there was a pool of water not far away.[23] A youngish Burman appeared a little later and confirmed the water so we set off with him and found a pool of muddy water surrounded with a fairly high tree covered banks about a mile away. We almost rushed at the water and drank with our hats while the Burman watched, we then asked him for food and he motioned us to come with him to his village. I was not prepared to trust [him] anyway so I refused and indicated that he should bring the rice to us, he went away.[24] We wandered round the pool and found a recently opened tin of tomato soup which I filled with water and drank because of the faint taste; on the west side of the pool we found a grenade and a webbing haversack with the right hand shoulder pierced, presumably by a bullet and a little blood stained. We then rested under the bank; shelling started about an hour later from the North-East presumably aimed at TOKSAN; it went on for some time sporadically, bits of shrapnel kicking up withers of dust in the field beside us; there was also no answering fire of any sort and when lying on the top of the bank for a time I could no human movement in any direction. We rested for about another hour but the Burman did not come back, and as it was getting towards evening I decided to move away from the pool and try and get to the river and work along its bank or nearby; I decided to do this because I was again uneasy both because of staying too long in one place and the Burman not returning and because the water might be a more frequented place by night. I followed the bed of a very small chaung making towards the river when we came out onto the paddy fields which immediately adjoin the river bank, a bullock cart which was going north turned round on seeing us, the driver galloping the bullocks until they were out of sight; that wasn't a very good omen but we continued to move towards the river rather foolishly across open paddy fields; we had got about halfway across when I heard a whistle behind me and turning round in fear and trepidation saw two khaki white men coming towards me while a few more were on the secondary bank of the river behind us; it was a patrol from KOYLI under FITZPATRICK who had gone out to pick us up as they had seen us leave the water-hole from GAUNGDAW-U, rather obviously two white soldiers and one probably an officer.[25] So that ended a very unpleasant day on my own. I have unfortunately forgotten the name of the man who was with me but I photographed him later. The patrol then returned in open formation to the village with myself in very high spirits, and once inside the village I reported to CHADWICK who listened carefully to all my reports of the enemy movement I had seen, as he sat against a fence and I drew in the dust to illustrate.

Bn was successfully lifted by 2 TANKS (7 Armd Brigade) to the area of TOKSAN, the tanks returning to the main road. After this there was no apparently no further contact with our forces. A wireless truck had been allocated to Bn HQ with I think Burman signallers (?) Apparently our duties were to delay the enemy on this flank as long as possible, as an enemy column had been reported on this area. Bn bivouaced in the area on the water pool where I was the next afternoon, and a man was left on the road near Toksan to contact the transport that was going to arrive during the night. Presumably the Bn "stood to" at first light, and on the first signs of action from our direction was sent into the attack by CHADWICK. I know very little of what actually happened, and that only from subsequently. The attack was apparently with two companies forward and one in reserve, they succeeded without much difficulty in driving off the enemy (consisting mainly of Burmans in blue uniforms with, I believe, a stiffening of Japs) who were very busy going through our transport and had failed to post guards, as they obviously had thought that when they drove HQ and guarding coy in rout, that they had disposed of all opposition. The Bn did not follow up the success, and presumably just went behind the nearest hedge, where they were joined by another coy or so and attacked again before we could get very much of the transport away. Bootland had his throat shot away while trying to drive a truck away with some Burmans actually on it, presumably by one of our own men.[26] Very little transport was saved, one truck filled with mortar amm which got stuck in a sunken road nearby, and about four carts, none of which had any food on, so that all the heavy weapons, food and amm was lost as well as tpt and baggage. The Bn then retired to the village where I joined them, and were left alone all day.

After telling all I knew, I looked round our positions to see how we stood, it was a typical bamboo constructed village, two or three empty mule carts lay in the central alley where they had been left after the mules had been unharnessed; there was no food in the perimeter except 'chuggery' and peanuts in small quantities and diminishing amounts of water in ordinary pottery jars. 'Taffy' PHILIPPS was glad to see me and gave me half a hard tack biscuit. I wandered about a bit and ate a few peanuts with a sergeant who I knew well as the evening gradually closed into the beginning of twilight. The usual stand-to took place, the men lining the thorn fence of the village; on the south side someone suddenly spotted a small Japanese patrol working forward towards the edge of the village from the direction of the waterhole, obviously trying to find out if the village was occupied, everyone was quiet and tensed up; but the cattle belonging to the village were used to being let into the village at sundown and stood round the gate on the northen side and lowed loudly to be let in, which sounded loud and hollow in the still and silent evening. I crept down to the southern side hoping to see them and knelt beside Chadwick, everyone had been cautioned not to fire even though they should come very close. Still nothing happened and whispered remarks from the soldier in front of me that they were out of the hollow to our immediate front and were gradually coming towards us; suddenly a rifle shot rang out, and the patrol immediately went for cover and disappeared. The tension was certainly removed but it was a blunder as the[y] definitely knew where we were. I went back to Bn HQ, it was now completely dark; David and I were both very tired so we lay down on a palm leaf mat and listened to CHADWICK working things out with WADDLEWORTH, the former wanted food and water in general but was particularly worried about the recce patrol as he was certain that there would be an attack within two hours. I was too tired to care really and only wanted to sleep. Anyway Chadwick ordered listening patrols to go out to the four corners of the village and out about two hundred yards, they were away about twenty minutes and returned to report movement of men and equipment and horses somewhere beyond all four points. So it was decided to move out quickly, three or four columns were formed quickly to leave at once on different routes. I went with Chadwick and David and the last column to leave; the few mules we had left were led with their harnesses on, but the carts were left. We left in single file and went slowly down the slope into the deeper shadows, little noise except the muffled footfalls in the dust and the jingle of harness; I was immediately behind David; we came to another hedge, halted for a short time and then slowly passed on and climbed through the thorns and jumped into a sunken roadway. After a short while we came to the village from which the noise of equipment had been heard and little fires seen; I could see them now through the hedge, about half a dozen very small cooking fires and as we passed I could hear the Japanese running to take up a position further into the village away from us. I carried a grenade in my left hand and a pistol in my right but nothing happened; they must have been surprised by our movements and probably thought that we were a patrol. I still think that we were lucky to have got away so easily. We walked on and on, halted as we lost direction, cut across country and down into another sunken track; one mule broke loose and ran away over the skyline to our left and kept galloping backwards and forwards near us. All the men were getting very tired besides thirsty as the majority had had no water for 24 hours. One man threatened to throw the Bren gun he was carrying away as no one had relieved him and David threatened him with shooting unless he did his duty, but the other men were ordered to take it in turns. Eventually we started walking on more level ground and I thought that I could smell water in the hot dry air which was making us all so weak. When we had gone about twenty minutes, someone looked round and exclaimed, I looked round at once and saw a [unreadable] of fire from where our village had been, the Japs had obviously fired the houses almost as soon as we had left, so we got out just in time. After ages more of monotonous plodding along a dusty sunken track, I began to smell water and after about another five minutes we came round a bend onto the sandy strip beside the chaung; all the men just ran across the road and fell on the water, drinking straight from the chaung, or scooping the water up in their hats and pouring it over their heads. There was hardly a sound except the dripping of water until the men slowly got up and struggled into line. Chadwick then started to look for a less vulnerable bivouac point, and we marched back about two hundred yards and branched west up a slight rise onto the top of a low hill overlooking the chaung. We had at once flopped down in a circle of about a hundred yards diameter with the remnants of the Bn HQ in the centre; guard was posted on each side and officers [were] awake in rotation.

April 15

Day adrift again beside the Irrawaddy. Rejoin Bn at Magwe well after dark, spent night there.

Bn formed up at first light and moved off down the hill to cross YIN CHAUNG,[27] I was sent ahead with three men as advance patrol. As usual went too fast and on locating the river, had lost touch with the main body; we then became very jittery and on tracing our steps back from the bank heard clinking of harnesses and thought that we saw bullock or horse carts in the dim light, our main body had no carts left so we sheared off at once and started to cross the river that was not more than six inches deep although about two hundred yards broad where we crossed; there was a steep bank on the other side, about ten feet, which we climbed and started to cross the waterlogged and marshy paddy fields which were in the immediate valley of the river as there were some slight hills; when we were about halfway across a machine gun opened up with two bursts, we were caught completely in the open and dropped to the ground immediately. I shouted at them to move by leaps and bounds, two got up and ran for about two hundred yards before dropping as another burst was fired, after that we got into the YIN CHAUNG river bed without further firing and no one hurt. I held a council and we decided to make for the river Irrawaddy as we thought the Japs would be well across the chaung further up and anyway it would not lead us north to our lines. My original intention was to find a boat, cross the river and make it up the other bank; when we got to the river, to our right seems unprepossessing and too exposed, on our left a high cliff which led onto an open beach on which I thought I could see a boat. It was still fairly cool and we made quick progress to the end of the cliff; I detailed a man to go and look at the boat which was lying not more than a hundred yards away along the beach, he went stayed a few seconds and returned, the boat was rotten and holed and was impossible to use. We rested for a while watching boats going backwards and forwards across the river from Myingan, This made me decide that the risk of crossing was not worth it as the other side was quite clearly occupied, whereas our side was allowing some freedom of movement. We became more and more hungry as some of us had [not] eaten for well over 36 hours, so the man who spoke Burmese took my kukri [and] went off to the nearby village way back from the bank, from which we could just hear animal noises, he went away and it became hotter and hotter. Somehow I had got hold of a book which I had read sometime before called "Death comes to the Archbishop", I remember trying to shelter from the sun under an overhanging tuft of grass and trying to read, but it was no use; I was still carrying my saw-off shotgun at this time, I didn't consider it a particularly good weapon to be caught with, so I took it apart and threw the bits in the river.[28] I was getting fidgety with hunger and heat so I moved off a little from the rest, higher up the cliff where I thought I could see a little piece of diminishing shade, I got there and sat down just below the top of the cliff and looked south down the river. I had not been there long before a Burman appeared and walked from about fifty yards away from me slowly [unreadable] looking intently as if searching, I crouched down and fortunately the others were silent and I think he went away without seeing anyone, but I wasn't going to take any chances as I always worked on the principle when anyone comes near, move on after he goes away as he must have seen you, I am quite certain that this is the principle reason why I am alive today. I clambered down to the others and we started to move up river once again, making very heavy progress in the heat, muddy and uneven ground, and to some extent all weakened except myself, as far as I could see, from lack of food. We gradually walked along back up the river, crossed the mouth where we had been earlier and started to go on further; but the bank became precipitous with no ledge between its base and the river, it was very very trying [unreadable] through at least a foot of mud all the time half in and half out of the water, the sun beating down all the time. It seemed hotter and hotter every minute, our bodies streaming with sweat, cloaked with mud and a heat haze dancing before our half closed eyes. I had decided to move on without the other man who had gone off for food because he had not come back within the prescribed time, I did not think we could afford to wait about after the appearance of the searching Burman. I was stronger than the other two and I kept on getting in front and having to stop; it must have been at least two miles of this extremely [unreadable] before we came to a break, a sandy slope leading to a small village MEBLADAUNG [inserted above the text], there were one or two boats at the bottom and one or two useless ones thrown up on the bank; I cannot remember if I saw anyone, but as the cliffs started again immediately after the break and we were in no condition to go on struggling half in and half out of mud and water; I climbed up the slope and across the open ground to the little group of huts about half-a-mile, round which a few people were moving. I made friendly signs when we came near and asked for food; they were friendly and said that food would be ready in about half-an-hour which they would prepare for us. They were kind to us, and we thankfully rested in their bamboo house taking off our stockings and boots, and generally pulling ourselves together; while the father of the house boiled a huge bowl of rice with vegetable seasoning. It soon arrived and I am afraid that the three of us polished off a very large bowl of rice in next to no time; they watched us avidly eating with interest; afterwards the other two went to sleep on the mat while I sat on the frame bed and rested, I was still nervous and uncertain and I was certainly not going to sleep so I just stayed awake and watched to see that nothing happened. All was quiet except for the movement of the children and cattle, and the evening cool gradually made itself felt so after they had rested for an hour I woke them and said we were going to move off so they started to pull their boots on. Meanwhile I talked to our host who asked my advice about his teeth which were loose and rotten with decay, I gestured that extraction would be less painful in the end but he equally vigorously gestured that he wouldn't. I then tried to make him take money for our very substantial meal but he vehemently refused although I tried to press him. I must remember to visit them again sometime. I did not think there was any point in following the river which was curving wildly so we set off north towards Magwe, we went along the flat river plain just to the left of a low line of hills running north to south which started about a mile from the huts where we had rested; just before them there was a stretch of fine sand and running across them were the very clear impression of Japanese two-toed boots which appeared to be quite fresh, I think that there were about three or four sets. I was very worried about this because unless we saw another set going the other way it meant that a Japanese patrol was between us and the river. The sun was nearly down now and I hurried them as we were following a narrow path along the riverside of the low hills, the ground on our left gradually fell away into a chaung filled with shallow pools of water, just before we came to the end of these low hills, I saw several men moving about outside a lonely hut on the other side of these pools, looked as if they were carrying boxes; I moved on hurriedly and soon the path sloped down a little and went between tall grasses or maize and occasionally even shallow chaungs, which ran deeply across the low lying river plateau. The others were getting more and more tired, and I tried to hurry them on but they continued to lag behind but in the damp still twilight I was getting more and more nervously alert and I gradually led the little party by about fifty yards, carrying my rifle cocked under my arm very much at the ready. We seemed to have walked a long way, when gradually the tall grass thinned away from us and the ground cleared into cultivation; we stopped at a hut nearby and drank some water out of a pot, and I asked the middle aged man who lived there the way to Magwe. It was nearly dark now and after a while we came to a newly destroyed village THINBAWZIEK [inserted above the text], still with piles of smouldering ashes and sheets of twisted corrugated iron, as we neared the place a bullock cart rumbled away hurriedly, the white shirted driver flogging the bullocks. We passed through the village and onto a tree-lined dusty road which forked a little further on, I had almost lost my sense of direction as I thought it was best to keep left and get onto the river, I'm afraid my common sense was rather [unreadable]. We went along the fork a little way and then turned off into the fields and we soon reached the river-bank. I left the Yorkshire private by the hedge and went off with the other bloke to recce, when we came back we couldn't find him so that we had to go on without him. I decided foolishly to walk up the bank until we bumped into someone, hoping it would be our men; across the river the oil lights of a large village were twinkling. We plodded up the bank making a hell of a noise on the loose stones, it was very dark because the trees on the seemingly high bank threw a shadow even with no moon. After a while we could see buildings on our right, KINYWA, [inserted above the text] but still no sound in the night; after another quarter of a mile there was an unintelligible challenge from high up on the bank and thinking it was Japanese as we couldn't recognise the language, we flattened ourselves, very very frightened; then someone switched on a torch and slowly swept the beach, we were quite obviously spotted so I stood up with my hands above my head shouting that it was a British patrol without much conviction; they kept the light on us until we were inside when we found that they were Burma Rifles; we had a drink with an NCO in a house nearby, he was British and after he took us to the Bn lines. We had an enormous meal of sausages and bread with beer having reported to Chadwick in a house nearby, and then went to sleep in the open with my pack as a pillow.

April 16

Leave MAGWE early; attacked in position on TAUNGDWINGYI road. Night above chaung north of MAGWE

We left Magwe early on the Taungdwingyi road in 3-ton trucks to take up position on milestone 340 about ten miles out of town; it was a cool morning and I rode in the front of the truck. I felt more elated and happy than I had for months. We soon arrived there and debussed, the mortars being put up on the south side of the road, I think for some unknown reason we all had a false sense of security. The two companies deployed forward and Bn HQ sat down in the ditch on the other side of the road to the mortars. Dublets of transport came through driving very fast, so CHADWICK decided that our lorries with the mortars ought to go in case they were road blocked as the road lay across our front to the west. They had been gone about ten minutes, when another string of about five lorries came down the road from our left, when they got about 150 yards to our left a concentrated group of mortar shells fell on the road in about fifteen seconds, the first truck caught a direct hit on the driver's cab and ploughed onto the grass verge burning furiously, another truck, apparently hit in the engine, stopped on our side of the road without burning, I don't remember seeing the driver at all but I gathered that he was alright. The driver of the exploded truck was dead with most of his side gone, one of our officers took his identity discs.[29] The next lorry after this swerved, braked for a while and then accelerated wildly, while an Indian who seemed to have been knocked off by the swerve, ran after it down the road screaming wildly to be picked up; the last lorry was just a chassis with a driver's seat and a white man driving, he drove past at terrific speed, I can still see his white, strained and staring face. I was still in the ditch beside David in the roots of a big tree, humming 'Dubarry' for some unknown reason, both of us watching the shells bursting on the road and the surrounding verge. There seemed to be little smoke from the bursts, just the crack and flash and the whisp of dust knocked up by the explosion; it was a strange scene, little noise except these mortar bombs and occasional bursts of small arms fire from in front, the little figures in the ditches and the tall thin column of black smoke from the burning trucks (the second one was set on fire and was irreparable). Chadwick began to worry about his flank position after about half-an-hour, and David lent me his binoculars and I crawled to the edge of the road and watched to our right across some shallow dead ground to a slight elevation about a mile and a bit away, but I saw no movement at all. Our position here was very unfortunate as we had apparently only received orders to take up position on the milestone, with no stated time of withdrawal or anything else; I believe that the 6th Bur Rif were to be responsible for passing on our withdrawal order but as we subsequently found out they had crumbled and broken on being attacked earlier that morning as they had been completely over-run and lost their identity as a unit; anyway at about 10 o'clock it was more or less apparent that very soon we would be over-run in a direct attack or outflanked equally thoroughly and destroyed. Before the attack had started a few of the remaining carriers under the command of a Capt. WILSON of the Bn seconded for other duty and come up from somewhere said that he would look into the position but we heard nothing. So Chadwick decided to retire northwards and accordingly passed the word to the two companies forward to retire at once in order; we waited impatiently while the runners went forward and when the two companies appeared straggling across the road to our left and right, we packed up and went with them; the fields were dry and powdered and it was heavy going and slightly uphill to a faint crest about a mile away; once we cleared the trees and cactus bordering the road, the Japs must have spotted us as there was the thud of a gun and the slither of a shell over our heads which burst with a flurry of dust about 100 yds to our left, I crouched instinctively but went on; everyone spreading out more and more in no semblance of order, another shell slithered and crumped near to us, but everyone went on. It was a nasty thing to walk away and leave one's back to the enemy, mentally unprotected. It was boiling hot by now and the slow trudge with no water except that which could be got hurriedly from villager's huts, was wearing the men down badly; so after about two hours we were over the rise and come down the road which led from Magwe to Yenangyaung just before the road fork to NATMAUK beyond the now derelict aerodrome. We rested for a while in the north ditch of the road, and David and I managed to get a drink from the 'chuglee' of an ordinance Sgt in Bde HQ that we knew. After a while the Bn remnants moved onto the road fork, halted for a while and then moved on up the wide edged road; KANBYA [inserted above the text]. I remember passing the Bur Rif Colonel from Magwe who was sitting in a little tin roadside shelter and wished him 'good morning'; he seemed to be in control of his Burmans who looked up to him and seemed well and happy. The Bn marched until just before mid-day and halted in a village to the right of the road where 'Taffy' Philipps and the remainder of the men who had got away in the trucks early that morning had prepared a meal.[30] Plenty of food and bread was provided, I think everyone had a square meal and was able to rest. I went through my kit inside the house for a while; someone loosed off a rifle through the floor, carelessness, but luckily no one was hurt; I went outside and took a photo of David and Waddleworth [photograph inserted in the diary] resting against a bamboo wall.[31] The village I think was called Kantha. I had not seen HOOD, my batman since the night in the surrounded village when he was with the Indian No.9; I could get no information about him from anyone except a somewhat vague rumour that he had developed VD and gone sick. I really do not see how he could have caught a dose (I saw him later at 17BGH Dehra Dun when he did not seem to be suffering from any visible malady.) Officers are supposed to have orderlies more for protection than anything else and as I had noticed RICHARDSON when he was in the officer's mess at YENANGAUNG when he was in the mortar Pl of Bn HQ and since there were no mortars nor any likelihood of there being again, and as he seemed a very cheeky sort of soul my age, I asked him if he would come with me; he said that he would like to so I asked FITZPATRICK the mortar officer and he agreed, so long as he could have him back if any mortars materialised. About the only thing that we found in any of these villages we rested in were buckets of 'juggery', the sugar made from the juice of the toddy palm, which was very tasty and I usually carried quite a lot in my pack whenever I could find it. We set off again in the middle of the afternoon but as the road was much used by cart traffic and wide and obvious from the air, columns of men were moving back on either side of the road about two hundred yards out; it was again heavy going, because there wasn't always a convenient track and to plough across the heavy dusty fields which were parched and cracked. After about two miles before the KADAUNG chaung we swung back very near to the road in the early evening just as part of 7 Armd BDE went past covering us with veils of thick dust; soon after that we swung away from the road again and started to go downhill in narrow twisting gullies. We halted halfway down for the normal ten-minute halt in the o-hour by the side of the gully when I took the photograph of DAVID MARTIN, CHADWICK and THROGMORTON [photograph inserted in the diary]. While we were resting some mounted Indian infantry went past us on small shaggy ponies. Towards the bottom of the hill we debouched onto the road again and some of the men managed to fill their water bottles at the well on the right hand side of the road. I remember that during the afternoon we had heard or seen a raid going on in the direction of KADAUNG chaung; this chaung has a particularly steep approach on the north side and very soft and yielding sand on the crossing, even though it had been reinforced with brushwood. The Bn crossed the chaung well spread out in case of sudden air attack; even when I crossed a truck was slithering and skidding across, on the steep assent on the other side there was a truck stalled on the left hand side of the road with a few machine gun holes in it.

We must have spent the night in that village. It was occupied by an Indian Mountain battery with mules which moved off in the afternoon. I had had my boots soled with rubber. It had become unstitched at the cap and this was sown up by the battery saddler. There was a motorcycle lying on the road. I tried to destroy it but the pistol bullet bounced off the petrol tank. I shot a goat with my 22 rifle and pushed it down the well to contaminate the water supply.

April 17

Day spent on march to YENANGAUNG. Night spent just south of oilfields. Night spent about 1 mile East of road junction leading to Yenangyaung. Was given whisky by the Brigadier but passed it to [batman] Richardson as I did not drink. Just before sun-down saw a launch on the distant river, some thought it was Jap. Did duty for David during the night, but fell asleep for a few minutes but luckily woke up quickly. Cool night. No events. Bivouaced about 10 yds S of road in a hollow. Area 185800.[32]

The oil tanks were burning. We filled our water bottles twice from 15 a cwt water lorry. A bottle of beer was produced for each man.

April 18

Day waiting for oilfields to be cleared. Moved late afternoon. Night in oilfields road-block. Night in Area 203845

The next day was very hot, with almost no shade on the low hillside. My head was in the shade, my body in the sun. My boots split again. Moved north into oil field as Battalion; everyone was very ragged. I carried two rifles for others. I took boots off a dead Indian, slightly too small. Slept on the ground with boots off. There was a sudden panic in the middle of night. Stood up shouting 'Stand fast KOYLI!' I never slept with my boots off again.

The next morning the Indian camp followers were fighting for water under a broken water pipe. A Jap recce plane came over low, circling, and was fired on by Bofors but not hit. We moved off eventually over Pin Chaung, it was only a foot deep but everyone stopped to drink again and again. A shell burst in the water upstream. We were drinking water for the first time in days. On the far side we walked through the abandoned Jap road block. A 25 pdr was firing south from near there, gunners stripped to the waist.

We were taken by lorry to a camp on the slopes of Mount Popa and there was a feeling of elation as we climbed up the slopes into greener trees and away from the dust. We stayed there maybe two nights with running water. I think by now we were reduced to twelve officers. I washed in water coming out of a pipe in the path side. We were lodged in new wooden buildings. I cannot remember seeing a single Burman but as we were waiting to leave just below the village washing place, some villagers offered us mangoes. I do not remember having any personal equipment except my small haversack and half a blanket.

The new QM was Stevenson ('Taffy' Philipps had died from a heart attack at the Pin Chaung crossing), a thin dark man who was eventually hospitalised in Dehra Doon with an ulcerated leg. We were talking about what would happen when we got to India and he said that they would probably all be sent to an Indian hospital as we were so dark from not being able to wash, and sunburn.

We were taken by lorry to Taungtha, a crossroads where the HQ was based in the rest house and compound. I erected a dummy anti-tank gun facing down the road with a piece of piping and boards. The Chinese came through in lorries with slaughtered pigs cut in half and tied on the side of the bonnet in some cases. One Chinese officer stopped for a time and he wrote me an identity card in Chinese. He was photographed with a group of us. Emptiness and silence of house awaiting an attack. A sort of social vacuum. Frightening. One concentrates on the turn as far as one can see down the road. Total yellowness.

I was sitting against the wall near a bullock cart and I saw Fitzpatrick and another soldier leading a column of Burmese, one of whom was carrying what looked like a keg of nails on his head. I heard some distant gunfire. I heard they had been shot as looters or spies. This later became a criminal investigation as a war crime and I was interviewed by two detectives from Scotland Yard. I told them frightened men are profligate with guns. From there it was a long, hard march with the HQ on the road, with parallel columns out on the sides providing cover. We were picked up by some tanks and the driver gave me a drink from his water bottle.

April 19

Japs attacked YENANGYAUNG from South. Cross PINCHAUNG in afternoon. Night beside old road block

Morning saw Bn troops moving around oil tank in area 201863 and shells bursting in YAGYIBIN area. Damaged tank concentration of vehicles and many wounded at rd junction 201856, also saw there OC.17 Div. On patrol in afternoon moved east down Taungbet chaung from 20484936

April 20

Picked up by Bn moving in morning to POPA Night there in camp

April 21

Day and night in POPA[33]

April 22

Night at POPA 22/23[34]

April 23

Night 22/23 Taungtha[35]

As we were waiting just below village washing place to move off first, villagers offered us mangoes. Trucks waited in field for us north of the village/walked there. Very crowded in trucks.[36]

April 24
Night 24/25 Taungtha

April 25
Night 25/26 at Taungtha

April 27
Chinese Div passing through us at Taungtha. David Blown up.[37] Night in rain near Myingan.

Passing through Myingan. Town deserted. What looked like single-storied factories were burning on our left at the beginning of town. 10-minute halt after that in the middle of a mango [unreadable] in which I sheltered on right of road under a balcony and smoked a cigarette. Haigh the vet officer had been carrying some extra food on his horse for me, but I took it off and gave it to the Bn despatch rider to carry. Bivouaced area K 8006 in a field. Track Myingyanto Myotha was dust only. I did not know that they were going to blow at [that] moment – I was nosing around in the Post Office looking for stamps when I heard a muffled bang. Richardson was upstairs, suddenly I heard a man running, I shouted, alarmed to Richardson and on going out saw the Cpl (on right on picture with Chinese Captain) with his clothing on fire staggering towards me.[38] He was too hysterical to talk properly, was white and blackened, I pulled the burning clothes off and got him up the road to Bn HQ, he was already shivering. Photograph below. On the upland beyong Taungtha, well before Myingyan. Bare, rocky. P8388[39]

We stopped at a small town. The post office was deserted with no stamps in sight. (My father was a collector.) The cinema contained an enormous dump of tinned foods. I took some tins of condensed milk to suck while marching but I did not know that they were going to blow it up. While I was looking round I heard a dull thud and did not think anything of it until I got back to the main road where I found Martin and two others badly burned and being sent off in a car. Martin looked the least badly burnt. They had tried to set light to the store of food with petrol and when it set alight a tongue of flame came out of the door and hit all three.

April 28

Marching all day. Crossed IRRAWADDY in evening. Night in Pungyi-chaung

Crossed river at Sameikkom. There was an inspection bungalow actually on the bank on the Mandalay side. We crossed in late afternoon. Very steep banks, and some ramps for embarking vehicles had been built of rough logs.

Crossed in a stem launch manned by Royal Marines. Disembarked on the other side through a metal scow and an Irrawaddy flotilla boat of some sort, on which there were some male [unreadable] who were presumably [unreadable] the boat. There was also a big case of bayonets lying open on the right of the plank onto the boat, presumably there for us to take, they were the short variety. Equally steep bank on the other side. Just off the edge there was an abandoned ambulance and I think a pile of unwanted engineer stores. It took us about half an hour to cross. The RMs were taciturn and uncommunicative, some were stripped to the waist and red brown. Villages on both sides were set back at least half a mile from the river, with a broad bare patch in between. About 2 miles from crossing, Div General beside path and said well-done[40]

The next day we marched all day and in the early night we marched through Myingyan. An eerie experience with the town completely deserted and some of the buildings on fire.

We halted in fields beyond the town and it started to rain but I just went to sleep in the open. I was too exhausted to care.

The next day, we marched down to the Irrawaddy at Sameikkon and crossed in motorboats run by Royal Marines. It took some time to get across and I was photographed on the stern of a Burmese river boat. We marched off in single file and a Burmese couple of men stood by the side of the track giving drinks of water out of a pot they held. I cannot think they were spies, for they would not have had to do that to count numbers etc. I dropped out of the line of march to drink, which I should not have done.

April 29

Resting all day and night at SAMEIKKON (PK8338)

Lay on a dais under a poongyi-chaung all day. Remember trying to reconstruct some of my lost poems in a little green paper backed note book. CQMS chasing chicken in p.k. compound. Animal killed and cut up on small table under p.k. Entrails left there. Area PK8240[41]

April 30

Move off in evening from SAMEIKKON. Night at [unreadable] village half-way to MONYWA

May 1

Marching. Right leg went lame. Night near CHAUNGU with transport

May 2

Bn moved off at dawn, transport at midday. Bomber CHAUNGU. Night on carts going round MONYWA

Somehow we now had bullock carts for carrying ammunition. They were parked in a village near where we stopped for the night and the village started to burn. No one seemed to want to get the carts out of the village so I pulled them out with another soldier. It was about that time that in the night I heard a group of soldiers referring to that 'fucking Tanner'. I thought it came from a corporal attached to the new Quartermaster Stevenson, who was reputed to have taken money from dead bodies before crossing the Sittang after the bridge was blown.

As we got near to Monywa there was firing there and the drivers of the bullock carts, which presumably were their own, by this time had disappeared. So we drove them ourselves. They would only go so far without water; I took my pair down to water. I slept on one cart, on the shaft between the bullocks.

May 3

Rejoin Bn in morning on YEU road. Night in village on left of road

After rejoining the battalion on route. Marching on left side of the road with slight embankment on the left, carrying TSMG with circular and mechanism done up in rags for protection. Jap recce plane came down from N very low, about 100 feet, with rear gunner standing up and machine gunning; had stopped firing by the time he came near me and was reloading. I was unable to get the rags off my gun in time.

Remember meeting Chadwick on coming across Bn and walking across to him on right of the road and wishing him 'good morning'.

Ambulance, British manned, waiting on road before Bn and I told the driver that there was a badly wounded Sikh in much pain on a bullock cart driven by another Sikh a little way back on the left.

After making a circuit round Monywa I rejoined Yeu road at a place where there was I think a level crossing and several blown-down railway trucks below the embankment on the right on the far side.

Big pagodas[42] were probably at E5780 near AUNGTHA[43]

We were all on the road north of Monywa and I met another KOYLI 2/LT in the middle of the road. I think he was a well known(?) rugger player and looked fit; I understood that he collapsed and died next day. The Jap plane was no more that 50 feet up. There was scattered rifle fire at it. At that time I was carrying a Thompson sub machine gun with a cloth round it to keep out the dust, but by the time I had got the cloth off, the plane had gone. It is a very awkward weapon to carry and I exchanged it with someone for a rifle.

May 4

Day resting: move off in evening towards YEU. Night on march, attacked.

Bivouacked for day in area PANGABYIN (E5003)

Attacked in BUDALIN at night (E5518)[44]

May 5

Still marching, very exhausted. Lifted by tanks and transport to YEU. Night in village beside canal

Went on ahead of Bn from bridge near KYAKAT (V9399) in army civil car sports model.

Notice on YEU blackboard telling everyone to collect 48 hrs rations. Arrived at village ahead of everyone else. R0424. Deep canal under embankments. New wooded bridge Ordered large chicken curry and rice from villagers. As troops began to arrive, villagers asked me if they ought to leave, I said no as their property would not be taken. Chicken was killed, skinned and washed in canal. Many troops passed through. One wireless truck on far side of village

Railway bridge at ZAWA (R0323)[45]

More marching along the road to Kaduma where a track led off towards Kalewa and the Chindwin. Some of us were in a patch of trees lining the road when Jap dive bombers came. I heard the dive starting and through the leaves could see a glint of an engine cowling as I clung to the earth. A string of bombs came down. The one on my left was about six feet from my outstretched arm and had not gone off but another on the other side went off and killed an Indian who was blown up against the next tree. This made me increasingly deaf on the right side. Their explosive was picric acid and this yellowish powder was blown under my finger nails. A very narrow escape. The bomb did not break into small pieces of shrapnel but into large peelings, eighteen inches long. I could not have escaped if it had broken into shrapnel.

Somewhere we were all inoculated against cholera with a large needle and syringe but I do not think there were individual doses; it seemed like a horse syringe to me. Also we had a visit from a C of E Chaplain and a group of about thirty stood around in a clearing singing from hymn books that he handed out, plus a few prayers.

At Kaduma which was the end of the proper road and the end of provided supplies, there were RASC or RIASC personnel handing out tins from piles of crates according to what you wanted to carry. I think I took tinned milk but I have a memory of marmalade, which would have been stupid to take. The road or rather track from then on was littered with thrown away kit.

I think I picked up then a surveyor's compass but it may have come from Yenangyaung. I carried it all the way to India. We were now on a dirt track but out of the trees, which could carry only one-way traffic. We were lifted as far as Pyingaing by lorries and I stole the food of the Indian driver from behind his seat. This was my last act of bad behaviour.

We saw an abandoned 15 cwt lorry in a river bed and managed to manhandle it up on to the track as it was in working order. The remains of 7th Armoured Brigade had gone this way and there was an abandoned maintenance van left beside the track with shelves of spares down the sides. A despatch rider went past and I noticed his shorts and leggings.

May 6

Start marching in afternoon, slow progress still exhausted. Lifted to and night at KADUMA

The Battalion rested all morning in the little village doing nothing; from early morning the troops in 17 Division which had concentrated for the night at or near MYINBAUK had moved out towards KADUMA, so that by mid day we were the only troops left. During the morning there was a loud explosion and a cloud of dust from the southern line of the canal which I took to be demolitions.[46]

May 7

Transported all day, minor breakdown but arrive in evening at PYINGAING. Night spent there.

May 8

All day resting. Night spent in shallow hole in the sand at PINGAING chaung.

At Pyingaing the Brigade was ordered to go north through forest tracks to the small oil field at Indaw and then to cross the Chindwin and over the mountains to Tamu. The other two battalions were Indian, with roughly the same number of men in each, the KOYLI probably the weakest at about 150 men all told. It was cold in the night and the half blanket was welcome; I slept in the sand of the Chaung which made an easy hole for my hip. Indian engineers had dug holes for water in the river bed to bring in the water. I think there was a petrol pump pulling the water out into a sunk tarpaulin.

I had maps then as the ones which I gave to the Regimental Museum have the miles marked off as we marched. I had torn off the parts which were not relevant to our march. We started before dawn and halted in the middle of the day, with each battalion leading in turn. After the track petered out we followed a stream bed and suddenly there was an American five-ton lorry in the gully, as it could go no further. In the village that we came on, on the other side of this divide there were people and I shot a cow running across a field, for which I paid the owner 100 rupees. It was properly cut up by a KOYLI who had been a butcher in civilian life.

Two men were missing next morning. It is very easy to disappear in war if someone leaves the group because no one will go looking for them. Perhaps they were murdered, There was boiled rice to eat and I shared a small tin of cheese with Richardson. The next day we marched to Indaw across a motorable track and we were told that there would be transport there to help us but there was not; only a number of deserted staff houses and a dispensary. The Brigade doctor was an Anglo-Burman whose equipment was all in a haversack which he carried. We went together to the dispensary to see whether there was anything useful but it had been looted. I took a tube of spray of local anaesthetic but I have no idea why.

The next day was hard as the motorable track followed the oil pipeline, which criss-crossed the river many times, often through eighteen inches of water. This was hard on already worn-out boots. One man was barefoot by now and he got a pair of brown shoes in a deserted store at the village on the banks of the Chindwin. There was an abandoned lorry among the houses.

Rumours are perhaps important in keeping people going in more or less hopeless situations. When we were marching beyond the Chindwin a large formation of bombers went over heading east and everyone thought they were RAF going to give them hell. All one could say was that from underneath the Blenheim and the Jap Betty do look much the same from 10 thousand feet below, but in fact these were Jap bombers returning from flattening Imphal. But thinking that they were RAF was a stimulus to keep us going.

About this time the wireless gave out; it could receive but not send. In this way we heard the news of the invasion of Madagascar. At least a day and night there and during this time a steamer came up the river and there were many reunions. Philipps the Commissioner of Mandalay was on it and was well known. At this place there was no crossing that connected with any track to India so we marched at night over a bend in the river. I held onto a pack strap of the man in front and went along sleep walking. The diary does not explain the extent to which everyone was not only exhausted but probably on the verge of malnutrition. At this stage we would have done better for water but it was never more than one meal per day of plain rice and whatever we happened to have carried from Kaduna, most of which had gone long ago.

May 9
Very early start; morning halt at PAWLAW. Night spent in CHINGCHAUNG.

May 10
Night at MAWTONGYI

May 11
Night at LAWTAR

May 12
Marching all day, arrive at PANTHA in the evening Night there in house on left of track looking W

May 13
Day resting at PANTHA. Order for moving received, night in same place.

May 14
Move off in early morning Bde crossing Chindwin all afternoon. Night at YUWA

At the crossing place we were carried over in small canoes paddled by Burmese, two or three of us at a time. There was at least one English-speaking Burman in this village, a civil servant who had worked at Mawlaik and I bought from him a small Burmese knife. We were smoking native tobacco by now. From then on it was a climb over a mountain range into the Tamu; for at least the top part there was a clearing through the trees and a single telephone line. It was slow progress as some Indian engineers were in front making it wide enough for mules. The mid-day halt was overlooking a river and Richardson washed something of mine. Some hornbills flew over the river to our right.

May 15

Early move. Night half-way up river at KYAUKCHAW

May 16

Morning halt before steep climb over hills. View into Assam. Night beyond YU river at HLEZEIK

Below supposed to be a view into Assam [referring to a photograph] 1st figure Throckmorton 2nd [Lieut.] Waddleworth.

Steep hill climb-halfway up halt.

One man collapsed at crest, Doctor went back but the man was dead. I was fairly far up in column and remember Dr passing back on my left. Wireless line to India over [unreadable] in a broad drive. Just after [unreadable two words] a bungalow set on right in some trees, like an I.B.

Climb after lunch, some people drunk from stream just after climb, one died probably. Slow descent. At least one halt on way down.

Passed one isolated empty house on arrival at level empty egg shells on a stick outside. Then [unreadable] empty village with some people watching us from the back. I believe that they reported that the village had been thoroughly looted by some refugees. We crossed river for night's halt. Grass hut full of empty tins just beyond crossing.[47]

May 17

False entry into TAMU and had to march back. Night spent three miles South of TAMU in woods.

May 18

Rest all day and night spent in the same place.

May 19

Still in woods, ordered sick in afternoon. Moved truck from CCS to PALEL through mountains.

Near the top I had to fall out because of the dysentery and as I squatted down I watched the column go by. I photographed swallow-tail butterflies drinking the salt on someone's knees when there was a halt near the summit, as someone had died. I doubt whether there were any who could have been classed as fit, but nothing could be done for anyone who dropped out; you walked or died.

Down at the bottom we went through Brigade HQ and its mules in a very narrow river bed, in which they had tried to dig for water in the bends. We went through a deserted village and into Tamu. There we found that the whole column should have stayed out at the foot of the hills as a flank guard. Some officer said to the Colonel acting Brigadier that it was not his fault. We were then told to march south clear of the refugee area and some of the men seemed to be in a bad way so I carried several rifles until we got into an area to camp which was free of the smell of dead refugees. A very sickly sweet smell. I saw no refugees.

That evening I was told to report sick with some others and after a cursory verbal examination by a doctor, went in a three-ton lorry to Imphal over the mountains via Palel; presumably my dysentery was more noticeable than I had thought but in appearance I doubt whether I looked any better or worse than the others. We must have driven all night over this winding narrow track but I remember nothing of it except that we got to Palel before dawn and slept in the open on flat rice fields. There was a supply depot in a tent and I got rations for the party but as there was no way to cook anything we ate the contents of the tins cold.

May 20

Moved in truck convoy to beyond IMPHAL in morning. Night in rough hospital beyond milestone 105

At Imphal there was a thatched roof hutted camp but it was raining. The latrines were a pole over a pit and not enclosed in any way. A field security corporal asked me for my identity card. We were all sent on to Dimapur where the hospital was overcrowded and over-worked. We were told if we could walk it would be best for anyone to get on the train, which was leaving that evening. Two of us helped a third man who could not walk very well but he was not in the KOYLI, to get to the train. I went to a canteen and bought some powdered milk for the journey and sardines.

The fourth man in the compartment was from the IV Hussars with a badly infected swollen elbow. I burnt a penknife blade with a match and sprayed the arm with the local anaesthetic that I had taken from the dispensary in Indaw and cut it open. This let the pus out and the arm got better during the trip. Many years later a man came out of a shop in Bognor Regis I was entering and it was this officer; his arm had given no further trouble.

We got to Patna and were put into a hospital. A family friend, my mother's godson, who was a legal officer, came to my bed and enquired whether I knew an officer called Tanner in the KOYLI – I must have looked awful. There was still the fear of deprivation as I queued for food twice and hid the second lot in my locker, where it went mouldy. I think I was four months in hospital before I was discharged and posted to the Intelligence School at Karachi. I was eventually invalided out to the UK in November 43, ending up in MI2d in the War Office dealing with Japanese non-divisional troops, for which I wrote the Periodical Notes in the series on the Japanese Army.

May 21

Moved off in late morning. Travelling all day to MANIPUR Road. Arrived in hospital late evening

May 22

All day in hospital, visit canteen. Move down to train by truck in evening.

May 23

Train moved off at dawn.

Copy of two pages from the diary of 2/Lieut. R. Tanner, 223473

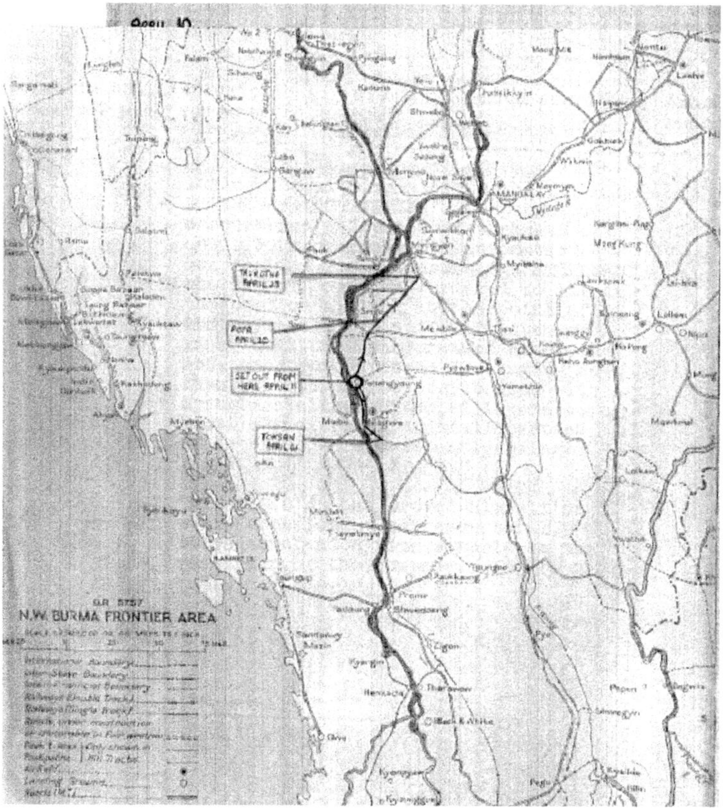

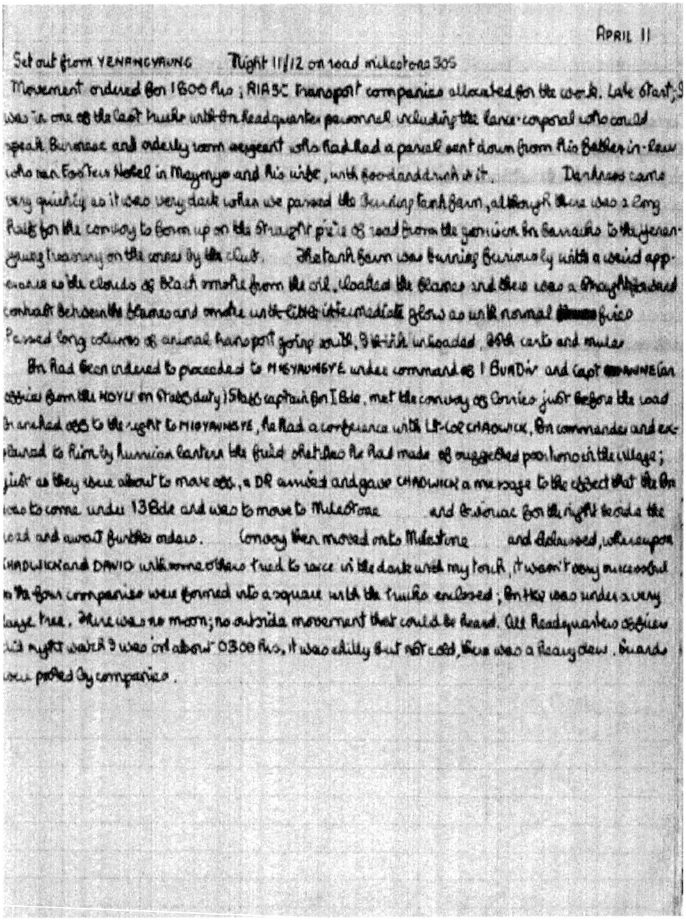

APRIL 11

Set out from YENANGYAUNG   Night 11/12 on road milestone 305

Movement ordered for 1800 hrs; RIASC transport companies allocated for the work. Late start; I was in one of the last trucks with Bn headquarters personnel including the lance-corporal who could speak Burmese and orderly room sergeant who had had a parcel sent down from his father-in-law who ran Fosters Hotel in Maymyo and his wife, with food and drink in it.   Darkness came very quickly as it was very dark when we passed the burning tank farm, although there was a long halt for the convoy to form up on the straight piece of road from the garrison Bn barracks to the Yenangyaung township on the corner by the club.   The tank farm was burning furiously with a weird appearance as the clouds of black smoke from the oil cloaked the flames and there was a straightforward contrast between the flames and smoke with ~~little~~ intermediate glow as with normal [redacted] fires

Passed long columns of animal transport going south, I think unloaded, AT carts and mules

Bn had been ordered to proceed to MIGYAUNGYE under command of 1 BurDiv and Capt [redacted]NE (an officer from the KOYLI on staff duty) Staff captain for I Bde, met the convoy of lorries just before the road branched off to the right to MIGYAUNGYE, he had a conference with Lt-Col CHADWICK, Bn commander and explained to him by hurricane lantern the fruits of the recce he had made of suggested positions in the village; just as they were about to move off, a DR arrived and gave CHADWICK a message to the effect that the Bn was to come under 13 Bde and was to move to Milestone   and bivouac for the night beside the road and await further orders.   Convoy then moved onto Milestone   and debussed, whereupon CHADWICK and DAVID with some others tried to recce in the dark with my torch, it wasn't very successful so the four companies were formed into a square with the trucks enclosed; Bn HQ was under a very large tree. There was no moon; no outside movement that could be heard. All headquarters officers did night watch I was on about 0300 hrs, it was chilly but not cold, there was a heavy dew. Guards were posted by companies.

Appendix B

Military Medal citation for Sergeant R. Steerment 4688224

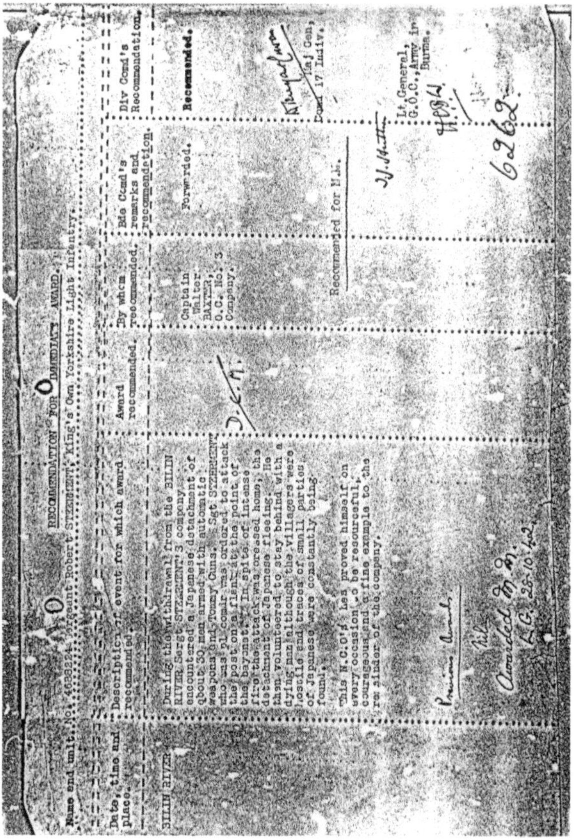

RECOMMENDATION FOR IMMEDIATE AWARD.

Name and unit. No. 4688224 Sergeant Robert STEERMENT, King's Own Yorkshire Light Infantry.

Date, time and place.	Description of event for which award recommended.	Award recommended.	By whom recommended.	Bde Comd's remarks and recommendation.	Div Comd's Recommendation.
BILIN RIVER	During the withdrawal from the BILIN RIVER Sergt STEERMENT'S company encountered a Japanese detachment of about 30 men armed with automatic weapons and Tommy Guns. Sgt STEERMENT who was pl comdr was ordered to attack the post on a flank at the point of the bayonet. In spite of intense fire the attack was pressed home, the detachment of Japanese fleeing. He then volunteered to stay behind with a dying man although the villagers were hostile and traces of small parties of Japanese were constantly being found. This N.C.O's has proved himself on every occasion to be resourceful, courageous and a fine example to the remainder of the company. Previous Awards Nil Awarded M.M. L.G. 28-10-42	D.C.M.	Captain Walter BAXTER, O.C. No. 3 Company.	Forwarded.	Recommended. [signature] Maj Gen, Comd 17 Indiv.

Recommended for M.M.

J.J. Hutton

Lt.General, G.O.C., Army in Burma.

H.O.W.

6262

Appendix B/1

Military Medal citation for Lance Corporal J. Howson 4689997

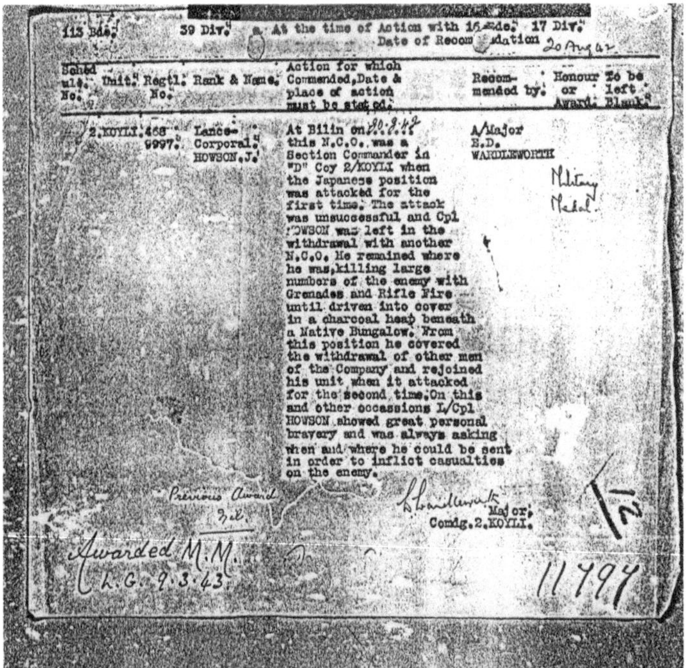

113 Bde. 39 Div. At the time of Action with 16 Bde. 17 Div.
Date of Recommendation 20 Aug 42

Schedule No.	Unit.	Regtl. No.	Rank & Name.	Action for which Commended, Date & place of action must be stated.	Recommended by.	Honour or Award.	To be left Blank.
	2.KOYLI.	4689997.	Lance-Corporal. HOWSON, J.	At Bilin on 20.2.42 this N.C.O. was a Section Commander in "D" Coy 2/KOYLI when the Japanese position was attacked for the first time. The attack was unsuccessful and Cpl HOWSON was left in the withdrawal with another N.C.O. He remained where he was, killing large numbers of the enemy with Grenades and Rifle Fire until driven into cover in a charcoal heap beneath a Native Bungalow. From this position he covered the withdrawal of other men of the Company and rejoined his unit when it attacked for the second time. On this and other occassions L/Cpl HOWSON showed great personal bravery and was always asking when and where he could be sent in order to inflict casualties on the enemy.	A/Major E.D. WARDLEWORTH	Military Medal.	

Previous Award Nil

Major,
Comdg. 2.KOYLI.

Awarded M.M.
L.G. 9.3.43

11797

Appendix C

Japanese Map of the actions between 9–21 April 1942

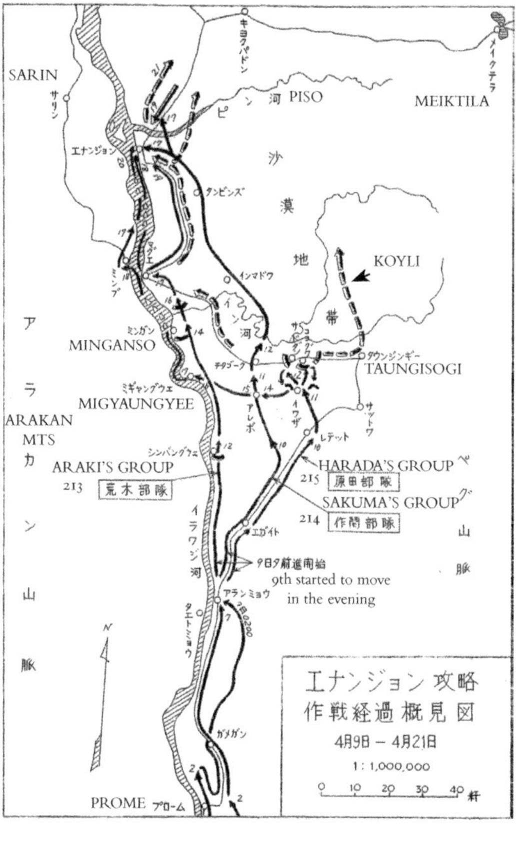

Source: 33 Division, 215 Regiment, Regimental History

Appendix C/1

Japanese Map of the actions between 16–21 April 1942

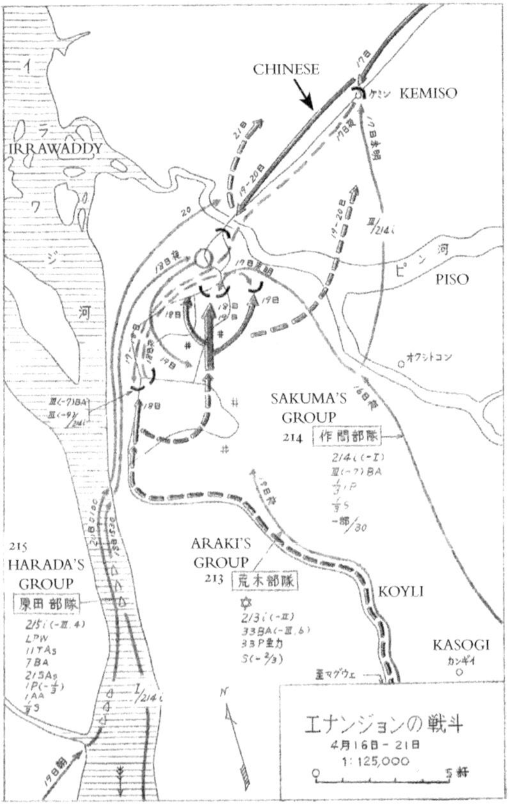

Source: 33 Division, 215 Regiment, Regimental History

Appendix D

Corporal John Heald's Roll

Corporal Heald's Roll was begun in Shillong, Assam, in 1942 and completed many decades later, after consultation with survivors and including the fate of POWs. It is a fascinating and sobering document and has been reproduced here word for word. It would be neither mawkish nor inaccurate to describe this list as a labour of love.

4689490 ABBOT J "BUD" DIED OF BURNS 20.5.42 AT SUPPLY DEPOT WITH MAJOR MARTIN + 3 OTHERS "A" COY

ABBOTT WALTER PTE (EX CPL) HULL, TOOK MESSAGE THRO 8 MILES OF JAP HELD JUNGLE, ATTACKED BY BURMAN'S SEVERED FINGERS OF LEFT HAND. RIGHT HAND DAMAGED DELIVERED MESSAGE SURVIVED "B" COY

ABLESON J.W. 2/LT KILLED AT WANETCHALLING 7.3.42 AFTER ONLY 2 DAYS WITH BATT, NO KNOWN GRAVE

ABRAHAM ERNEST MT SECTION EVACUATED ILL

4689109 ACKROYD C. L/CPL MULE DRIVER KILLED 8.3.42 NO KNOWN GRAVE

4689010 ACLAND CHARLIE L/CPL POW 23.2.42 ESCAPED LAST MONTH'S OF WAR CLARINET BAND, BATT, FOOTBALLER EMIGRATED NEW ZEALAND

4689701 ACOMB D. L/CPL MISSING 18.2.42 NO KNOWN GRAVE

4687888 ADDY A BUGLER "C" COY WOUNDED YENANGYAUNG

4698819 AINSON GEORGE PTE

4690604 ALDERSON J. PTE POW 19.6.44 SURVIVED

4689698 ALLSOPP R. PTE KILLED 23.2.42 "B" COY NO KNOWN GRAVE

ANNE "QUEEN" LT ATTACHED BRIG, H.Q. YENANGYAUNG

4689792 APPLEYARD V.T. PTE POW 23.2.42 SURVIVED

4689057 APPLETON J.R. PTE LEG AMPUTATED SITTANGE RIVER3" MORTAR SECTION NO KNOWN GRAVE

4690539 APPLETON J PTE WOUNDED IN ACTION

4684802 ARMITAGE A. BAND (HANTS) PLAYED CLARINET

4690322 ASHCROFT "JOEY" PTE POW, SURVIVED DOUBLE BASS BAND

4689012 ASHFORD R. PTE MISSING 23.2.42 SURVIVED

4689254 ASHKEW J.S. PTE MISSING 18.3.42 NO KNOWN GRAVE

4689157 ASHMORE JACK PTE MEDICAL ORDERLY – QUALIFIED NURSE

4690540 ASHTON T.W. PTE WOUNDED IN ACTION

ARUNDEL "DARKY" L/CPL SURVIVED BURMA SHOT DEAD BY ONE OF OWN MEN IN NORMANDY

AVERY CPL MANE FROM BILL SLEE MM + DCM

AYRES H.B. 2/LT KILLED NO KNOWN GRAVE

ADAMS SGT NAME FROM B. MEE

4689193 BAILEY H BAND KILLED YINON ROAD 18.2.42 NO KNOWN GRAVE

4695991 BAILEY ERIC PTE (LEEDS) MISSING 14.4.42 NO KNOWN GRAVE

4695992 BAILLIE G. PTE MISSING 15.5.42 NO KNOWN GRAVE

BACON PTE NAME FROM BILL SLEE

4689601 BARBER G.A. PTE MISSING 18.2.42 NEVER LOCATED
4689564 BALCOME C. L/CPL MISSING 15.5.42 NO KNOWN GRAVE
BAKER KEN PTE PLAYED OCORINA TO MULES SURVIVED
4695995 BARKER LESLIE (BRADFORD) FOOT WOUND 23.2.42 SURVIVED
4687506 BARROW JACK L/CPL (LEEDS) SAXAPHONE BAND
4695948 BARTLE H. PTE KILLED 3.7.42? NO KNOWN GRAVE
4689819 BARTON PTE (ROTHERHAM) JOBY BATMAN TO CAPT BAXTER "B" COY
4690157 BATTENSBY E. (LEEDS) POW 23.2.42 SURVIVED
4689188 BAXTER W. "WHIPLAST" LT LATER CAPT, C COY
BAXTER G.S. CAPTAIN C.O. "B" COY SHOT THRO, ARM BY BURMANS NR HLEGU
4688975 BAXTER H. L/CPL MISSING LATER LOCATED
4682216? BAXTER JOHN PTE (LEEDS) TROMBONE BAND, EMIGRATED CANADIAN MOUNTED POLICE AS SGT.
BEAUMONT R. (LEEDS) KILLED
BEDFORD MICK BATT, CHAMPION 100YD + 200YDS
4690131 BELL G. PTE REPORT DEAD 19.6.42 NO KNOWN GRAVE
4692822 BELL L. "TAGGY" PTE (HULL) MISSING 18.3.42 LOCATED
4689768 BELLAMY C.H. PTE DIED INDIA 26.5.42
4689233 BENSON J.A. SGT (YORK) SPOKE URDU AND BURMESE
BENSON FRIEND OF ERIC GILL, BENSON MARRIED PTE CLEGG'S SISTER
BEST JOHN M.M. SGT JOINED V FORCE
BETTERIDGE PTE (LEEDS) SQUAD OF FEB, 1937
4689088 BIGGIN F. CPL DIED IN HOSPITAL 15.4.42?

4685023	BIRCH A.T. "ATTY" SGT SIGNAL SECTION
1893496	BIRCH R. PTE MISSING 15.5.42
4689163	BIRD C.A. CPL MISSING 18.2.42 NO KNOWN GRAVE
4536283	BOOCOCK R.E. POW 23.2.42 SURVIVED
	BLACKBURN EDDIE MAYBE BURMA
4689744	BOOTH ERNEST "GENERAL" (LEEDS) WOUNDED 18.2.42
4684186	BOOTLAND A. SGT. SHOT THRO. JAW SURVIVED DIED 19—
	BORTON L/CPL "B" COY MAYBE BURMA MAYBE BARTON
	BOWES PTE NAME FROM JOSE ISAAC'S
4690110	BOYCOTT D.T. PTE MISSING 23.2.42 NO KNOWN GRAVE
	BRADSHAW PTE
	BREAM G, PTE ENLISTED MAYMYO DROVE TRAIN THATON
4690351	BOYLE D.T. PTE MISSING 17.5.42 NO KNOWN GRAVE
	BREWER G,C, PTE KILLED NO KNOWN GRAVE
4690271	BREWER R. BOY (WAKEFIELD) DIED 14.2.42 NO KNOWN GRAVE
4689812	BROOKS.R. PTE MISSING LOCATED
4689848	BROOKS.L. L/CPL WOUNDED 18.2.42
	BROOK JOE PTE (HUDDERSFIELD) REJOINED BATT, OIL FIELDS
4689414	BROOKSBANK H, L/CPL MISSING 23.2.42 NO KNOWN GRAVE
4691155	BROWN T.L. BOY (INDIA) TROMBONE IN BAND
	BROWN "SUGAR" PTE RATION STOREMAN
108389	BROWN H. CAPT POW SURVIVED
4689976	BROWNING L/CPL (WAKEFIELD) SQUAD OF FEB 1937
4688657	BROUGHTON G. SGT KILLED BY SNIPER 28.4.42
	BROADBENT BOB DISPATCH RIDER

4690884 BROXHAM H. PTE POW, SURVIVED

BRYANS L/CPL ANGLO/BURMESE ENLISTED MAY-MYO

4687309 BUBB W.H. PTE WOUNDED DIED 9.8.1978

4691029 BUCKLEY KEN PTE POW NO KNOWN GRAVE

BUCKLEY BOB CPL INCIDENT WITH BREN GUM OIL FIELDS

4689453 BURDETT W. L/CPL MISSING 18.2.42 NO KNOWN GRAVE

4688018 BURGIN G.W. PTE DROWN 23.2.42 NO KNOWN GRAVE

4696017 BURKE W PTE MISSING LOCATED LATER

4689100 BURKS F PTE MISSING LOCATED 19.5.42

4689745 BURROWS KEN, PTE LEG WOUND TOKSAN SURVIVED

4685620 BUTLER J.A. M.M COMS STEADED NATIVE DRIVERS

BUTCHER SGT. "B" COY NAME FROM BILL SLEE

BLACKBURN EDDIE

4689754 BUTLER JIM FERRIER (SCUNTHORPE) POW MARRIED FRANK STOTT'S SISTER

BARREN "GEORDIE" BENNY MEES BEST FRIEND

4696020 CADE HAROLD (DEWSBURY) WOUNDED 18.2.42 DIED 1992

4689639 CAHILL MICHEAL PTE MISSING LOCATED

CAHILL PATRICK PTE BROTHER TO MICHEAL SURVIVED

4692860 CALLADINE H. PTE MISSING 23.2.42 NO KNOWN GRAVE

4689180 CATON E CPL POW MORAL BOOSTER TO FELLOW POW'S

CARR "FLOSSIE" PTE LEG AMPUTATED SURVIVED

CASH PTE (DONCASTER) "C" COY SGT AFTER BURMA

4689720 CASEY M. PTE (LEEDS)

CHADWICK GEOFFREY O.B.E. LT/COL

EVACUATED MALARIA REJOINED BATTALION AS C.O. 17.3.42 TO IMPHAL

74720 CHADWICK CAPT, WITH 262/KOYLI JOINED CALVERT

CHAMPION PTE SAID TO BE A HYPOCHONDRIAC

CHRISTMAS PTE MULE SECTION KILLED WITH MULE 23.2.42

CLARKE MAJOR R.A.M.C. DESPERATE AMPUTATIONS AT SITTANG

4688839 CLARE E. PTE MISSING – LOCATED 8.3.42

4688782 CLARRE F. SGT DIED HAND TO HAND FIGHTING AT BILIM NO KNOWN GRAVE

CLARK "NOBBY" (BOLTON)

CLAYTON FRANK (BARNSLEY) BATMAN TO KEEGAN

4535540 CLEGG B "PUGGY" PTE WOUNDED IN ACTION

4689489 CLIVE W.A. PTE MISSING – LOCATED 8.3.42

CLUETH JACK "BOB" A ROUGH DIAMOND FROM K.O.S.B'S

COATES "MAGGIE" CPL REGIMENTAL POLICE

4689306 COCKSHOTT CLIFF PTE (LEEDS) KILLED 26.4.42 AT YENANGYAUNG NO KNOWN GRAVE

4691884 COCLIFFE CHRIS SGT NOT IN RETREAT BUT IN WINGATES CHINDITS 1943 LATER CAPTAIN

COCRANE PTE

COLES JOHN PTE (BARNSLEY) A SALVATION ARMY MAN SURVIVED DIED – 12–1992

COLMAN "BERTIE" PTE (BIRMINGHAM)

4690124 COLLINS CHARLES PTE (BRADFORD) KILLED LONE BAYONET CHARGE NO KNOWN GRAVE

4689704 CONNELL C. L/CPL (DONCASTER) ALONE REPAIRING SIGNAL LINES MISSING NO KNOWN GRAVE

4685957 COOMBS G. CQMS DIED IN WIFE'S ARMS ON WALK OUT WITH FAMILIES 1.5.42 NO KNOWN GRAVE

COOPER LITTLE KNOWN OF HIM

4689442 CORCORAN J. PTE KILLED 11.3.42 NO KNOWN GRAVE

4689761 COVELL A. L/CPL CAPTURED REPAIRING SIGNAL LINES RELEASED BY GURKHA PATROL KILLED 14.4.42 NO KNOWN GRAVE

100547? COX W.S. PTE DIED 18.4.42 NO KNOWN GRAVE

COOK "BOOMERGY" PTE SURVIVED KILLED IN FRANCE

4589204 CRABTREE F. PTE (SHIPLEY) LAST CASUALTY OF RETREAT COLLAPSED AND DIED 6 HOURS FROM PROMISED LAND, NO KNOWN GRAVE

CRANFIELD G.C. LT MISSING NR TOKSAN NO KNOWN GRAVE

4688337 CRAWFORD A.J. (LEEDS) SURVIVED

6202162 CRITCHER W. PTE DIED 17.4.42 NO KNOWN GRAVE

CRAVEN JOE BATMAN TO LT/COL BECHER

4689412 CROOKS ROGER (SHEFFIELD) DIED 1992

4692592 CROSS T PTE MISSING 25.4.42 NO KNOWN GRAVE

8464987 CROSSLAND "TOJO" (BRADFORD) WOUNDED SURVIVED FROM

4689486 SQUAD OF FEBRUARY 1937

4691299 CROSSLEY J. PTE ACCIDENTAL DEATH 4.11.42? NO KNOWN GRAVE

4689059 CROUGH A. PTE (S/SHIELDS) POW SURVIVED

4696265 CRYER L, PTE CARRIED HEAVY ANTI-TANK RIFLE FELL BEHIND – MISSING NO KNOWN GRAVE

4688131 CRUMMACK CPL A.A. PLATOON AT MAYMYO

CANNON TOMMY PTE GREAT BOXER

CORKWELL GEORGE (HALIFAX) SAME RAFT AS G HAWKE THEN JOINED RED CAPS

4690581 DADDY R.E. "RED" SAXAPHONE BAND POW, DIED RANGOON JAIL 8.6.44 NO KNOWN GRAVE

DAIGHTON "LEN"

4688775 DALBY "CHUCK" SGT REGIMENT POLICE – WOUNDED

4689119 DANFORD H. SGT (ROTHERHAM) KILLED NR HMAWBI 8.3.42 NO KNOWN GRAVE

4690525 DANFORD AW PTE POW 23.2.42 SURVIVED

4696046 DALANEY GERRY C.S.M. (PONTEFRACT) SWAM SITTANG IN HIS TIGHT UNDERPANTS

DALANEY PTE WOUNDED AT SITTANG SURVIVED

4685615 DARBY HARRY CQMS (SHEFFIELD) SURVIVED

4689824 DAVIS C. PTE BAYONET WOUND BILIN SURVIVED

4695887 DAWSON BILL PTE (DONCASTER) LARGE BULLET WOUND IN SHOULDER, JAP CAME AMONGST WOUNDED KILLING THEM OFF BILL SURVIVED

DAY PTE KILLED WITH HIS MULE SITTANG

DESFORGES PTE FROM GROUP OF 50 1941

DARWELL PTE A STRANGE BUT TRUE STORY

4688530 DIAMOND G, PTE MISSING – LOCATED 5.5.42

4689189 DIBBERT G.S. PTE DIED HOSPITAL 23.8.42

4689549 DICKINSON "C" COY

4689352 DIDSBURY JOHN L/CPL (N/SHIELDS) WOUNDED AT SITTANG SWAM RIVER

4689164 DIDSBURY RALPH PTE (N/SHIELDS) BROTHERS

4690096 DING J.W. PTE MISSING LOCATED LATER

4690971 DIXON E.P. L/CPL (GUDINSOME) WOUNDED DIED POW 15.10.52

4690901 DOE JOHN PTE JAP BULLET SPLIT HIS RIFLE BARREL

4536944 DOHERTY JIM CPL (BILLINGHAM) INDIA C.S.M.

DOLMAN J. CPL INSTRUCTOR SIGNALS SEC. MARRIED JAPANESE

DONNELLY J. DEKHO OBITUARY 1989

DORAN BOB L/CPL (LIVERPOOL) "B" COY

4681028 DOWNS W. W.O.2 MEDALS DONCASTER

4689367 DOWNING E, L/CPL POW 2/BATTALION?

DOYLE JRI CAPTAIN BULLET IN GROIN SURVIVED

DRIST C.S.M. NAME FROM BILL SLEE

4695886 DRURY J PTE (DONCASTER) MISSING – LOCATED
DUFFY C.S.M. FROM FEBRUARY 1937 SQUAD
4695888 DUKE HENRY PTE MISSING 18.2.42 NO KNOWN GRAVE
4689415 DURDEY C, PTE WOUNDED IN ACTION
DYSON J.R. W.O.2. MEDALS DONCASTER
DRANSFIELD BENNY SGT (ROTHERHAM) CARRIED CAPT DOYLE TO SAFETY THEN SLEPT
EDWARDS J. SGT WOUNDED BY NERVOUS SENTRY WHO KILLED H. ORGAN AT SAME TIME, NR YINON ROAD
4688455 EDWARDS A PTE KILLED SITTANG NO KNOWN GRAVE
ELIAS JACK PTE KILLED SITTANG NO KNOWN GRAVE
4687889 ELLIS "CHARLIE" PTE
ELSOME JACK (DONCASTER) DIED 1992 DEKHO! OBITUARY
4696057 ELSWORTH RAY PTE (LEEDS) BROUGHT HOME JAP FLAG
1438702? ELY R.W. PTE (LIVERPOOL) POW SURVIVED
4690432 EMMETT PTE (BRADFORD) L/CPL MALAYA
4690473 EVANS A. L/CPL POW 1.6.42 SURVIVED
EXLEY FROM CPL DOHERTY'S SQUAD
ETHERINGTON "ZEB" PTE
FARR "PADDY" NAME FROM BENNY MEE
FALL R.H. C.Q.M.S. MEDALS DONCASTER MUSEUM
4689427 FALLOWS (DONCASTER)
4694373 FARMERLY GEORGE (CONISBOROUGH) DROVE LAST BREN CARRIER OVER SITTANG BRIDGE
4690171 FENN A.E. "FINGERS" PTE UNFLAPABLE FENN VERY COOL IN ACTION – SURVIVED
4689081 FISH G.N. PTE DIED MALARIA 10.4.42 NO KNOWN GRAVE FROM THORME NR DONCASTER

4684294 FISHER A. CQMS ON RAFT HALF WAY ACROSS SITTANG – PANICKED – SWAM BACK POW DIED 4.10.1981

4534574 FITZPATRICK M. SGT WOUNDED 2.3.42

160575 FITZPATRICK GERALD 2/LT (LEEDS) JOINED BATT. HLEGU

FINNEY J. (S/LONDON) DEKHOI! OBITUARY

4688434 FLEMING T CPL DIED INDIA 5.6.42

4689407 FELTCHER JAMES A. CPL (YORK) C.S.M. IN INDIA

FLETCHER FRED PTE "C" COY BROTHER TO JAMES

4696065 FLEETWOOD H. PTE MISSING 18.2.42 NO KNOWN GRAVE

2573882 FOGG S.J. PTE MISSING LOCATED LATER

4689051 FOSTER REG. L/CPL DIED A POW 19.6.44 (LEEDS)

4690347 FOWLER HARRY (HULL) DIED EARLY 1992

FOX CPL M.M. SWAM FOR ROPES TO TIE TO DAMAGED BRIDGE STAYED IN WATER TO HELP NON-SWIMMERS WITH L/CPL ROEBUCK

FOX C.A. CAPTAIN SUFFERED POLIO ATTACK PUT IN CHARGE OF WIVES AND CHILDREN FOR EVACUATION INDIA

FOZZARD PTE (LEEDS) HAD STALL LEEDS MARKET

FRAMTON C.Q.M.S.

4688744 FRANCE C. L/CPL MISSING 13.4.42 NO KNOWN GRAVE

4690113 FRANCE P. "FROGGY" MISSING 23.2.42 NO KNOWN GRAVE

4689490 FREEGARD C. BANDMAN DIED POW

4693834 FREEMAN TED PTE POW YENANGYAUNG ESCAPED LAST MONTHS OF WAR DIED MORECAMBE 1993

4688658 FREEMAN SGT. WOUNDED

4687613 FRETWELL "BULL" (LEEDS) SURVIVED – MY M.T. SGT DEOLALI INDIA

4689767 FROST K. PTE DROWNED 23.2.42 SITTANG RIVER NO KNOWN GRAVE

4689696 FUNK L.E. SGT. WOUNDED 23.2.42

GRACE NAME FROM BENNY MEE

4695493 GARDNER W PTE WOUNDED MISSING LOCATED

4689692 GASCOIGNE HARRY PTE (PONTEFRACT) GRAVELY WOUNDED RESCUED BY A. MATTHEWMAN SURVIVED LONG JOURNEY FROM SITTANG

4690611 GASCOINGE D. PTE WOUNDED 12.3.42

GATES PTE "GINGER" (FEATHERSTONE) "A" COY

GAZE J. H.Q. COY DEKHO OBITUARY

4696074 GIBLIN J.M. PTE MISSING 9.3.42 DIED POW 12.9.42

4694057 GIBLIN E. PTE DIED ACCIDENTLY INDIA 19.6.42

4690100 GILL C.A. PTE DIED IN WATER WELL THATON NO KNOWN GRAVE

4689470 GILL ERIC (DONCASTER) "C" COY CROSSED SITTANG WITH RIFLE FURTHER UP RIVER

GILL GEORGE PTE NAME FROM E. MUSTILL

4535883 GILPIN J PTE SURVIVED DIED MALAYA FROM SCRUB TYPHUSS 25.7.1949

4687851 GLEDHILL "ZANK" SHOT BY SNIPER 23.2.42

4689945 GLEDHILL "GINGER" PTE (BATLEY) POW SURVIVED BROTHER TO SGT ABOVE

4686122 GODDARD E. PTE MISSING 13.3.42 NO KNOWN GRAVE

4748560? GOLDTHORPE J. "CURLY" C.S.M. DIED 31.12.1979

4689813 GOODWIN N. L/CPL MISSING 18.3.42 POW

4688746 GRAHAM N. L/CPL NAME FROM PHALLAS SURVIVED

4690720 GRAVES J. PTE MISSING 23.2.42

GRANVILLE GEORGE

GRAYDON ARTHUR (HALIFAX) DIED AUSTRALIA 1988 FROM DEKHO! OBITUARY

GREEN H.M. CAPTAIN "C" COY FOUGHT FULL CAMPAIGN FROM START TO FINISH

GREEN "CHICK" L/CPL "B" COY

4689720 GREENWOOD G. L/CPL POW 23.2.42 WENT MAD – DIED POW NO KNOWN GRAVE

GROTH LT (BRADFORD) FROM GROUP OF 50

GROUCH SGT. HQ COY SURVIVED

5677820 GROVES D.H. PTE DROWNED 22.10.42

4695857 GROVE W. PTE DIED 8.4.42 NO KNOWN GRAVE

4690720 GROYES J. PTE POW SURVIVED

GUEST B. C.S.M. (BARNSLEY) BURIED SILVER

GILES RON (HARROGATE) KEN BURROWS FRIEND

4694860 HAIGH J. PTE (BRADFORD) POW SURVIVED

4690712 HAIGH W.A.L. PTE MISSING 19.6.42

4696084 HALL A.W. PTE (ROTHERHAM) KILLED YINON ROAD 2.2.42 NO KNOWN GRAVE

HALL LES SGT (LEEDS) SURVIVED

HAGUE D.C. 2/LT JOINED BATT HLEGU 5.3.42

4696083 HALLAS PHILLIP "TAFFY" (HUDDERSFIELD) A WONDERFUL MAN DIED AUGUST 1994

HALLOWS "GINGER" ASSISTED E. MUSTILL TO RESCUE WOUNDED CPL HARRISON

4686844 HAMMOND T. "BOB" L/CPL

4688843 HANSON W.G. L/CPL SAT ON RIVER BANK AWATING CAPTURE – NON SWIMMER – SURVIVED

HARNESS PTE

HARWOOD (NEWCASTLE) FEB 1937 SQUAD

4689321 HARRIS P.M. L/CPL SHOT HIMSELF NR YENANGYAUNG TOTAL EXHAUSTED TO AVOID CAPTURE – NO KNOWN GRAVE

4689690 HARRISON B. CPL LAY WOUNDED IN OPEN AT DANYINGON – RESCUED BY HALLOWS/MUSTILL

4688955 HART J. CPL MISSING 19.2.42 NO KNOWN GRAVE

4690149 HARTLEY J. PTE KILLED LAST DAY OF WAR IN GERMANY

HAUGHTON W.G. MAJOR KILLED BILIN

4692730 HARRISON S.K. L/CPL

HAWKSWORTH BENNY (PONTEFRACT)

HAWKE "SPARROW" "B" COY

4689722 HAWKSWORTH T. PTE WOUNDED

4690461 HAWKINS PERCY L/CPL (DEWSBURY) POW DIED 1980

4696097 HAYKIN A PTE DIED POW 18.9.43

4689268 HEALEY DOUG CPL (DONCASTER) "D" COY PUSHED WOUNDED ON RAFTS AT SITTANG

7885143 HEALY EDWARD PTE MISSING 19.2.42 NO KNOWN GRAVE

4689269 HEALY JACK PTE POW SURVIVED

4692675 HEATH J. L/CPL KILLED NO KNOWN GRAVE

4690657 HASELGRAVE J. L/CPL MISING 19.6.42 DIED

2059603 HELSTRIP R.J.PTE (BRADFORD) WOUNDED

4692823 HEPWORTH W. L/CPL KILLED 18.2.42 NO KNOWN GRAVE

HENSBY C. (SHEFFIELD) DEKHO! OBITUARY 1992

4691060 HERBERTS K. L/CPL POW – SURVIVED

HELLIWELL "CHINNY" SHOULDER WOUND ENLISTED 16.5.1935

4695866 HEWITT TED PTE (DONCASTER) FITZPATRICKS SQUAD

4537227 HEWITT WALTER PTE MISSING 23.2.42 NO KNOWN GRAVE

HIELD BROTHERS ALL PTE'S FRANK, PAT, ANOTHER

4691026 HILL J. "TICH" BOY SOLDIER CORNET BAND EMIGRATED AUSTRALIA – DIED 1988

4695868 HILL SAM PTE (OSSETT) POW SURVIVED

4690144 HILLYARD BILL (REDCAR) GAVE HIS WATER BOTTLE TO WOUNDED SGT BOOTLAND – DIED 16.4.94

HILL JIMMY (LEEDS) MULES DIED 1993 (B. MEE)
4689084 HIRST J. SGT (DONCASTER) CAPTURED AS A CHINDIT 10.5.43 DIED POW 16.5.43
4689187 HISCOX J. PTE CLARINET BAND POW ESCAPED JAPS RETURNED HIS BOOTS SAID HE DIED OF A FEVER – NO KNOWN GRAVE
4689185 HOBSON F. L/CPL WOUNDED
HOGAN JAMES (LEEDS)
HOLDSWORTH PTE WAS A BATMAN
HOCKER 2 BROTHERS NAMES FROM B. SLEE
HOLGATE RALPH NAME FROM B. MEE
4690408 HOLLINSHEAD (MEXBOROUGH)
4690959 HOLMES A. PTE KILLED 15.4.42 NO KNOWN GRAVE
4690667 HOLMES J. "BOMBER" (BRADFORD) BOXER – POW 23.2.42 SURVIVED DIED DEKHO! OBITUARY 1987
HOOD BUGLER ESCORT FOR WIVES AND BATMAN TO TANNER
4688450 HOOLE J. CPL (WAKEFIELD) POW SURVIVED
4692702 HORTON "SNOZ" J. PTE WOUNDED SURVIVED
4689075 HORNSBY T. SGT MISSING 18.2.42 NO KNOWN GRAVE
HOTHAM CAPT. "C" COY
HORROBIN 2/LT NAME FROM FITZPATRICK G.
4690154 HOUGHTON BERT PTE (SHIPLEY) FEB 1937 SQUAD
4684604 HOUSLEY BILL C.S.M. (SHEFFIELD) "A" COY – KILLED BILIN HAND TO HAND FIGHTING NO KNOWN GRAVE
HOWDEN R.A.B. CAPTAIN 3" MORTAR SECTION LEG AMPUTATED AT SITTANGE – SURVIVED
4689997 HOWSON JOHN M.M. CPL 25 YRS BEAFEATER
4692789 HUBY R PTE DIED 8.5.42 NO KNOWN GRAVE
4689697 HUGHES R. PTE DIED POW 5.8.43 NO KNOWN GRAVE

4691149 HUTCHINSON H. PTE (SHEFFIED) WOUNDED HAND

HURLEY "POP" PTE ( ) MULES – SURVIVED

4688712 HYOMES G. SGT (DEWSBURY) POW – SURVIVED

HYMAS A. "BUD" (SCOTLAND) DIED 1992

4694790 HYSLOP W. PTE KILLED NO KNOWN GRAVE

4688782 HOFFMAN "VON" ARTHUR JAMES DIED SINCE WAR WAS A GERMAN

HOLGARTH "DANNY"

4696299 ILES GEORGE PTE (YORK) KILLED 20.5.42 NO KNOWN GRAVE

IRWIN FROM GROUP OF 50 MAYMYO 1941

IRVINE D. (HUDDERSFIELD) M.T. SURVIVED

IDLE "SUSSTY" PTE KILLED TESSLE WOODS NORMANDY

IBBOTSON A. 2/LT JOINED BATT, 5.3.42 AT HLEGU MISSING NO KNOWN GRAVE

4696106 ISAAC'S JOSE PTE (LEEDS) SURVIVED

IVES N. BUGLER NAME FROM F. STOTT

IZON A. (PONTEFRACT) DEKHO OBITUARY

4689771 JACKSON "JACKO" W. CPL (BARNSLEY) COOK SHOT IN ELBOW DANYINGON, MISSING NO KNOWN GRAVE

4686675 JAMIESON SGT. NAME FROM P. HALLAS

4690270 JARVIS "JACKIE" (BRADFORD) M.I. ROOM SURVIVED

JENNINGS CPL. P.T.I.

JENNSEN PETER SGT ORDERLY ROOM

4684826 JEWSON H. SGT DIED 21.10.42 IN ASSAM

836321 JOHNSON W. SGT (YORK) WOUNDED, STRETCHER CASE, PATROL CAME BACK FROM HIM BUT SGT WAS MISSING NO KNOWN GRAVE

JOHNSON EDDIE (LEEDS) GROUP OF 50

JOLIFF 2/LT WOUNDED, GAVE VITAL INFORMATION THEN DIED, NO KNOWN GRAVE

4690150 JONES PTE KILLED 18.2.42 NO KNOWN GRAVE

4692717 JOWITT SAM PTE DIED POW 26.6.44
4689099 JUSTICE JIMMY CPL "B" COY DIED 1961 AT STRENSALL BARRACK YORKSHIRE
KEEGAN JACK D.S.O. LT/COL GRAVELY WOUNDED SITTANG 23.2.42 SURVIVED DIED 1993
4689430 KELLSALL (LEICESTER) NAME FROM H. WEAVER
4690424 KELLY J.J. PTE DIED 17.2.42 NO KNOWN GRAVE
4690554 KELLY S. PTE DIED NO KNOWN GRAVE
KIBBLER BILL (SHEFFIELD)
4689290 KILBURN A. CPL MISSING NO KNOWN GRAVE
2821096 KILNER D. PTE (BARNSLEY) DIED 15.1.42 MALARIA TAKAW NO KNOWN GRAVE
KING "CHUTA" PTE DIED TYPHUS
4689016 KELIEY (SWINDON) NAME FROM H. WEAVER
796524 KIRKBRIGHT H. CPL DIED 27.3.42 NO KNOWN GRAVE
KNAGGS G. PTE MULE TRANSPORT
LAFFAY BATTALION GOALKEEPER
4687147 LANE G. "LUPE" CPL HELP TO MAKE RAFTS FOR WOUNDED AT SITTANG
LAWRENCE A. 2/LT JOIN BATT 5.3.42 HLEGU
4689668 LAWRENCE "NIGGER" CPL EUPHONIUM BAND WOUNDED 18.2.42
4689556 LAWSON B. (YORK) NAME FROM H. WEAVER
4689789 LAWMAN W. SGT "A" COY WOUNDED
LAWTON SGT WOUNDED
4690651 LAUGHTON E.V. PTE DIED POW 9.3.43
LAUNCESTON CECIL (LONDON) PRECUSSION BAND DRUMS
LAVERICK "JOHNNY) 2/LT LATER CAPT + ADJUTANT
LEACH B. "BUSTY" SGT (LEEDS) E^b CLARINET BAND LATER C.S.M. IN GERMANY
4689721 LEE G. "JIGGER" M.M. PTE (DEWSBURY) WOUNDED SURVIVED, M.M. IN EUROPE LONE CHARGE

ON MACHINE GUN NEST KILLED 3 GERMANS

4696124 LEE G.W. PTE KILLED 15.4.42 NO KNOWN GRAVE

4688494 LEE H.E. PTE MISSING

LEGO B.

4688791 LEIVERS JOE PTE (NOTTINGHAM) DIED POW 24.6.44 AFTER EATING WILD FRUIT

4695497 LENG A. PTE MISSING – LOCATED 19.5.42

LEVESLEY THOMAS MEDALS DONCASTER

4689126 LINDLEY GEORGE CPL MISSING – LOCATED 17.5.42

4690219 LINDSEY G. PTE DIED A POW

4690034 LOADER G.M. PTE WOUNDED

LOBBAN "DANNY" (BRADFORD) SURVIVED – DIED IN CARAVAN FIRE 1967 NR MANCHESTER DIED A PAUPER

4688831 LOCKWOOD ERIC PTE C. THOMPSON'S STEP BROTHER SURVIVED DIED 1980'S

LUMB L/CPL (BRADFORD)

4688254 LYNCH "PADDY" PTE

LYONS BENNY CPL PLAYED CORNET BAND

LYONS "TIGER" PTE (TAUNTON) SHOT DOWN JAP PLANE

4689350 MAGOWAN BEST FRIEND WAS HOFFMAN

MACANDREW (LEEDS) NAME FROM B. VAUSE

4693443 MACDONALD W.A. L/CPL ONE OF TWO ANGLO BURMESE BROTHERS WHO'S MOTHER MARRIED E. ROWLEY – W.A. WAS KILLED AT BILIN 18.2.42 NO KNOWN GRAVE "A" COY

MACDONALD BROTHER TO ABOVE

4691028 MCDONALD JOHN (BRADFORD) TENOR SAX BEST MAN FOR H. WILSON WEDDING

MCCLUNG SGT HEAD OFFICE?

4696128 MCCULLEY J. PTE MISSING – LOCATED ALSO SERVED IN EUROPE

4691125 MCEVOY D.S. PTE POW 23.2.42 SURVIVED

3053889 MCGORY J. PTE KILLED 23.2.42 NO KNOWN GRAVE
4689426 MCGOVERN GEORGE L/CPL (YORK) "C" COY
MCCORMACK PTE
MCKILLOP W. 2/LT JOINED BATT, 5.3.42
4695792 MAY T. PTE MISSING – LOCATED LATER
4695845 MAJOR JIM O.B.E. PTE (NR DONCASTER)
MALONEY PTE (DONCASTER)
MARRIOT BANDSMAN HELPED ON PERCUSSION
4688251 MARTIN S. "SOSS" PTE (SHEFFIELD) POW BEST FRIEND HANSON
COULD BE MARTIN J.C. BANDMASTER (HANTS)
SAME MAN MARTIN DAVID MAJOR ADJUTANT BADLY BURNT WITH 4 MEN – DESTROYING SUPPLY DEPOT ALL 5 MEN DIED
MARSH J. 2/LT JOINED BATT. 5.3.42 HLEGU
4689066 MARSH F. PTE MISSING – LOCATED LATER
4689409 MARSH J.F. CPL (BARNSLEY) POW SURVIVED
4689626 MASON E. "GYPO" (MEXBOROUGH) SIGNALS
4689430 MORRIS T. PTE DIED 6.1.44
MALLERSON "B" COY
MASKILL NAME FROM B. VAUSE
4688372 MASSIE J.W. L/SGT BUGLER KILLED BILIN NO KNOWN GRAVE
MANNION EDDIE MAYBE NOT IN RETREAT?
MATTHEWS W. PTE (SHEFFIELD)
4689781 MATTHEWMAN ALBERT CPL FEB. 1936 SQUAD SURVIVED BURMA – ON NORMANDY LANDINGS "D" DAY WITH GREEN HOWARDS, LOST LOWER LEG AT BAYEAU
4745049 MEE BENNY SGT (LEEDS) MULE AND MORTAR FITZPATRICK'S SQUAD
4689969 MEE KENNY PTE NOW CHELSEA PENSIONERS HOSPITAL LONDON "C + D" COY

4695792 MAY T. PTE MISSING OFFICIALLY DEAD SURVIVED

4686166 MENDUM C. L/SGT MISSING NO KNOWN GRAVE

4690428 MICKLEFIELD J. PTE (CASTLEFORD) DIED 25.5.42 NO KNOWN GRAVE

4691204 MIDDLETON F. PTE DIED 3.8.42

MILLER FRANK "DUSTY" C.S.M. COMMISSIONED IN CAMPAIGN SURVIVED – BOXER

4689571 MILLS N. PTE DIED POW 18.8.43 NO KNOWN GRAVE

4689424 MILTON (HALIFAX) NAME FROM H. WEAVER

4695796 MILLEA T. PTE (KILKENNY) COULD HAVE COME HOME DEC 1941 – DIED OF WOUNDS 7.5.42 NO KNOWN GRAVE

MIDWOOD H. (HUDDERSFIELD) DIED 1980'S

MITCHELL FROM E. MUSTILL

MITCHELL PTE (LEEDS) GRAVELY WOUNDED JAPS MURDERED HIM UNABLE TO WALK SEEN BY E. FREEMAN POW.

7886780 MOORCOOK K.L. PTE MISSING, NO KNOWN GRAVE

MOOREY BANDSMAN (BIRMINGHAM) PLAYED SAX – KILLED

MOOREY BANDSMAN TWIN BROTHER ABOVE PLAYED CLARINET KILLED

4689166? MOORE (HALIFAX)

MORGAN P. L/CPL (N/SHIELDS) MILITARY POLICE AT MANDALAY

4688954 MORHAMMER F. SGT FORMER NAME BRANDAN, WAS A GERMAN, MAY HAVE DIED AT SUPPLY DEPOT FIRE, CAME FROM FRENCH FOREIGN LEGION

4689176 MORRIS W.J. PTE MISSING LOCATED

4688528 MOULES R. BANDSMAN DIED OF WOUNDS 23.2.42 NO KNOWN GRAVE

4691990 MURREY PTE WOUNDED 18.2.42 NO KNOWN GRAVE

4696145 MUSTILL ERNEST PTE (LEEDS) WOUNDED AS

HE RESCUED WOUNDED CPL HARRISON AT DANYIN-GON – SURVIVED

4690993 MUSTILL HARRY PTE (LEEDS) COUSIN TO ABOVE WOUNDED WITH ERNEST

MYCOCK D.H. PTE NAME FROM G. FITZPATRICK

4690989 MYTUM G. PTE (LEEDS) POW SURVIVED

NASH (DONCASTER) NAME FROM W. DAWSON

NESDIN CPL NAME FROM H. WEAVER

NEWTON "C" COY

4688976 NEWSOME H. SGT DIED 27.8.42 NO KNOWN GRAVE

4696146 NAYLOR ALF, CPL (LEEDS) POW SURVIVED

4690541 NEVILLE J. "A" COY WOUNDED 13.3.42 SURVIVED – DIED 1990

4689680 NICHOLLS J. PTE WOUNDED 18.2.42

4690172 NICHOLSON G.D. CPL (DONCASTER) MISSING LOCATED LATER

4688827 NOBLE G. PTE MISSING LOCATED

4536150 NOLAN J. L/CPL DIED 23.5.42 NO KNOWN GRAVE

4685346 NORCLIFFE S. C.S.M. MISSING 7.42 NO KNOWN GRAVE

4689717 NORTHERN L/CPL POW 23.2.42 SURVIVED

NORTHFIELD PTE (SHEFFIELD) FEB 1937 SQUAD

4695806 OATES DEREK PTE (BATLEY) KILLED BAYONET CHARGE, BILIN NO KNOWN GRAVE

O'GRATH DANNY NAME FROM B. VAUSE

OAKLEY B.V. 2/LT JOINED BATT, 5.3.42 HLEGU

O'CONNOR 2/KOYLI

4610506 OLDCORN CHARLES C.Q.M.S. (BRADFORD) DIED POW 26.6.44 (MISSING 10.5.42)

OLIVER G. "GORDIE" SGT THIGH WOUND SURVIVED

4690972 ORGAN H.G. PTE (HULL) SHOT DEAD BY NERVOUS SENTRY NO KNOWN GRAVE

4689736 OWEN J.H. PTE WOUNDED
PADGETT L/CPL NAME FROM B. SLEE
PALPHRAWAND L/CPL (HULL) WOUNDED
4689423 PATTERSON (BARNSLEY) NAME FROM H. WEAVER
PARLE PTE DIED FEB 1993
4688779 PARKER "DON" PTE BREN CARRIER DRIVER
4695812 PARKER "LES" (LEEDS) POW 18.2.42 SURVIVED
4690111 PARKIN G.E. PTE DIED OF WOUNDS POW 7.5.42
4689734 PARKINSON S. PTE MISSING 23.2.42 NO KNOWN GRAVE DISPATCH RIDER?
2047016 PARRISH R. PTE (BRADFORD) POW 18.2.42 SURVIVED
PEARCE PTE BEST PAL TO E. DUKE
4695817 PECKSTON JIM PTE (LEEDS) "THE PENNILESS DUKE" DIED 16.4.1992
4690658 PEDDER E. PTE MISSING LOCATED LATER
4689228 PERROW C. PTE ACCIDENTLY KILLED 29.3.42
PHILLIPS "TAFFY" CAPT. BATT Q.M. AFTER 3 MONTHS HARD CAMPAIGNING HE QUIETLY SAT DOWN AND DIED, WITHIN SIGHT OF INDIA
PICKELTON R. (TYNESIDE) DIED 1987
4690659 PILBROW W. PTE MISSING LOCATED LATER
4689808 PINCOCK J. (S/YORKSHIRE) DIED 1984
4686647 PLACE E. "SWANEE" SGT MULE SECTION A FINE SOLDIER, TRAGIC END – DIED 1965
4689607 PLOWMAN T. PTE POW 24.2.42 SURVIVED
4690944 PRESCOTT J. PTE POW 24.2.42 SURVIVED
POGSON PTE SAID TO HAVE ONLY ONE EYE?
POOLE "TAFFY" CSM NAME FROM B. VAUSE
POOLE R.G.C. BRIGADIER WITH BRIGADE HQ?
4690213 POLLARD S. PTE MISSING 14.2.42 DIED 14.4.42 NO KNOWN GRAVE
4690711 PORTER A. PTE KILLED LATER AS SGT, CHINDITS 22.3.44 NO KNOWN GRAVE

	POPE N.S. 2/LT NAME FROM G. FITZPATRICK
	POVEY "GINGER" L/CPL
4689410	POWELL WILSON (LEEDS) MISISNG NO KNOWN GRAVE
4690145	POWELL WALTER (KNOTTINGLEY) ENLISTED 23.11.1936 MEDICAL ORDERLY, MILITARY POLICE AT SIEGE OF KOHIMA
4688699	POWIS CPL JAPS + CHINESE FIRED ON HIS SECTION AT YENANGYAUNG
4690189	PRESTON MALCOLM PTE (DEWSBURY) WOUNDED
4688132	PRICE FRED CPL (YORK) BROTHER TO DAVID
4689198	PRICE DAVID "KITNA" ALSO WITH CALVERTS V FORCE, KILLED IN MALAYA 1948 24.4. HAPPY PARK CEMETERY TAIPING
	QUINN L/CP (SHIPLEY) MAYMYO 1939
4353614	RAFTER J. PTE MISSING LOCATED
4689751	RAMSDEN A.J. PTE WOUNDED
4689078	RAMSDEN "BERT" BAND DOUBLE BASS, MISSING 26.4.42 NO KNOWN GRAVE
4696161	RATCLIFFE GEORGE PTE (LEEDS) POW 24.2.42 ALLOWED TO SKETCH LIFE IN + OUTSIDE RANGOON JAIL FOR JAP COMMANDANT
4690158	REDMILE W. PTE DIED POW 10.9.42
4685112	REVILL FRANK SGT. (SHEFFIELD) DIED POW 26.7.44 NO KNOWN GRAVE
	RENTON S.S. 2/LT JOINED BATT 5.3.42 HLEGU
4695771	RICHARDSON T.J. (GOOLE) BATMAN TO CAPT TANNER
4695772	RICHARDSON CHARLIE (LEEDS) WOUNDED
4827440	RICKLETON "BOB" SGT (NEWCASTLE) DIED 1988
	RIDDLE W.L. 2/LT JOINED BATTALION 5.3.42 AT HLEGU KILLED BURMA 1944
	RICKETTS N. (W/BROMWICH) DEKHO OBIT

4689810 REID PTE DIED POW 9.2.44
4690516 RILEY HARRY PTE WOUND, NOW TOTALLY DEAF
RILEY CQMS DIDN'T LIKE BEING CALLED "DOCCA"
RIMMER R.E.O. 2/LT JOINED BATT 5.3.42 AT HLEGU, 5 DAYS TIED ON MULE SLEEPING SICKNESS AT LATER PART CAMPAIGN
ROBINSON MAJOR M.C. ASSIST NON-SWIMMERS TO CROSS ROPES TIED TO BROKEN BRIDGE MAYBE DUKE OF WELLINGTON REG.?
4696166 ROBINSON G. PTE MISSING 18.2.42 NO KNOWN GRAVE
4689420 ROBINSON G.E. PTE (BRADFORD) DIED POW 30.9.44 NO KNOWN GRAVE
4689168 ROBINSON WILLIAM CPL (N/SHIELDS) REPORTED KILLED AT PROME – SURVIVED
4689166 ROBSON E. PTE (GATESHEAD) DIED PROME HOSPITAL
4696165 ROBERTS S. PTE DIED POW 19.2.42
ROEBUCK L/CPL M.M. (LEEDS) HELPED NON SWIMMERS AT SITTANG
ROEBUCK BROTHER TO ABOVE
ROSE TOMMY CQMS H.Q. COY
4699709 ROSE VICTOR PTE (NEWCASTLE) DIED 1990
ROSENDORF "ROSIE" FROM GROUP 50
4688686 ROTHERHAM W.L. PTE MISSING LOCATED
RODGERS PTE
4681786 ROWLEY TED (SHEFFIELD) BROTHER TO JACK BELOW – LATER TED WAS KILLED 29.3.45 IN EUROPE AS A SGT.
4688659 ROWLEY JACK L/CPL WOUNDED 8.3.42 NEVER FOUND AGAIN, NO KNOWN GRAVE
4690956 RUDLINGTON H. CPL MULE DRIVER WOUNDED
4691003 RUDSTON A. PTE KILLED 10.4.42 NO KNOWN GRAVE (SHEFFIELD)

4542342 RUKIN DENNIS PTE (BRADFORD) POW DIED NOVEMBER 1991

RYE "DRUMMER" (NEWCASTLE) NAME FROM B. TIGHE, ALWAYS DRUMMING FINGERS ON ANY-THING

4690522 RYLAH E. CPL MISSING 23.2.42 NO KNOWN GRAVE

SARGINSON (SHEFFIELD) BROTHER TO T. KILLED FRANCE CAEN 1944

SENIOR

SAFFE ANGLO INDIAN

SALT F.J. (DERBY) DEKHO! OBITUARY 1988

4689712 SANDERSON G.V. L/CPL (SHEFFIELD) POW 14.4.42 SURVIVED

SARGINSON T. (SHEFFIELD) BULLET INSIDE LEG

SELLARS 2/LT NAME FROM G. FITZPATRICK

4689261 SELLARS (ROTHERHAM) FROM H. WEAVER

4694864 SEWELL B. PTE (BARNSLEY) WOUNDED 12.3.42 DIED JUNE 1ST 1990

4696175 SCARGILL G. PTE MISSING – LOCATED

4689257 SCOTT J. PTE (BRADFORD) MISSING, LOCATED

SCOTT W. PTE DIED 1992 DEKHO OBITUARY

4536326 SHAW H. PTE KILLED NO KNOWN GRAVE

4688956 SHAW G. L/CPL WOUNDED

4689646 SHAW T. PTE (S/KIRBY) MARRIED MAYMYO 16.5.1935 DIED 30.7.42 BURMA

4689699 SHARPE R. PTE POW SURVIVED HID UNDER ROOTS OF TREE AT SITTANG

4696184 SHEARD N.A. PTE (HUDDERSFIELD) DIED POW 11.1.43 DISENTRY

4695784 SHELDON LEN L/CPL MISSING 12.2.42 DIED POW 1.2.43

4696181 SHEPPARD G.H. PTE MISSING – LOCATED

SHIPLEY G.A. (EDMONSTON) DIED 1985

SIDEBOTTOM LEN (SHEFFIELD) FEB 1937 SQUAD SURVIVED ACCIDENTAL FALL INDIA

4693537 SIMPSON W. PTE MISSING LOCATED DAMAGED HAND WITH GRENADE
4695788 SLATER E. PTE (BARNSLEY)
4613941 SLEE BILL PTE (NEWCASTLE) WOUNDED LATE IN CAMPAIGN
4690571 SLOW R. L/CPL KILLED NR YINON NO KNOWN GRAVE
5047415 SHENTON "TOMMY" (STOKE) 3 PLATOON "A" COY SOUTH TAFFS
4264775 SHORT "GEORDIE" PTE
4689691 SIMMS ARTHUR PTE (LEEDS) FROM H. WEAVER
4688842 SLIDE C. PTE KILLED 23.2.42 NO KNOWN GRAVE
SKINN JIM (DONCASTER) SURVIVED
3698266 SMITH D. L/CPL KILLED 3.4.44
4690535? SMITH R. BIG STRONG MAN SAID TO HAVE GONE DOWN TO 6 STONE SURVIVED
4696179 SMITH GEORGE PTE (LEEDS) "SMUGE" DIED 9.6.1988 LOVED HIS MULE CALLED "TOMMY"
4696174 SMITH JOHN PTE (LEEDS) BROTHER TO GEORGE ABOVE, UNABLE TO CROSS SITTANG, SMALL PARTY LIVED ON JUNGLE FOWL SURVIVED
4689705 SMITH H.B. PTE (NORMANTON) POW SURVIVED
SMITH ERIC PTE (DONCASTER) DIED 1990
4691785 SMALES (WAKEFIELD) DIED 1989
4690474 SMYTHE J.J. L/CPL DIED JUNE 1942 MANY MEN OWE THEIR LIVES TO THIS BRAVE CPL, NO KNOWN GRAVE
4695737 SNOWDON H. PTE WOUNDED DIED 1980'S
SOUTH J. SGT MT SGT
STONE BOB (LEEDS) FROM H. WEAVER
4690985 SPEIGHT W. PTE DIED POW 10.11.42
4695740 SPENCER ALBERT PTE MISSING
4692798 SPENCER F. PTE DIED POW 7.1.43
SPIBEY TOMMY PTE
4684329 SPINDLEY F. CQMS DIED OF WOUNDS, NO KNOWN GRAVE

	SPOONER BERT PTE (LEEDS) JOINED MIKE CALVERTS V FORCE LATER MADE MAJOR
4695742	SQUIRES C. PTE WOUNDED
4691580	STAFFORD J. PTE (SHEFFIELD) LEG AMPUTATED AT SITTANG DRAGGED ON BLANKETS TO RIVER BANK 41/2 HOURS CROSSING PUSHED AND PULLED ON RAFT BY 5 MEN, SURVIVED
4689718	STANLEY W. SGT MEDALS DONCASTER MUSEUM DIED 1987
	STEVENS V.L. 2/LT JOIN BATT, 5.3.42 AT HLEGU
4696199	STEAD G. PTE KILLED NO KNOWN GRAVE
4689537	STEAD HARRY L/CPL DISPATCH RIDER SHOT BY SNIPER AT THATON NO KNOWN GRAVE
4695744	STANDIDGE W. PTE (DONCASTER) DIED 8.11.41?
4688224	STEERMENT R. SGT M.M. STIRLING RECORD
4682599	STEEL W. SGT (TAUNTON) DIED 1989
4684365	STEVENSON J.S. MAJOR MEDALS DONCASTER
3130485	STIER "JOCK" LEN PTE (BARNSLEY) POW SURVIVED ALSO SERVED IN MALAYA 1947
4691030	STOTT FRANK BOY SOLDIER POW SURVIVED
4689598	STEVENS G. PTE POW DIED 1972
4692932	STUBBS G. (PONTEFRACT) MISSING 12.3.42 NO KNOWN GRAVE
4690146	SPINK JIMMY (PONTEFRACT) ENLISTED 23.11.36
4689707	SWAIN T.W. PTE KILLED 9.4.42 NO KNOWN GRAVE
4690530	SYKES D. PTE DIED 5.8.42
4695752	SYKES H. PTE DIED POW 9.10.42
	STOCKBURN FRED KILLED IN ACTION
	STRAW
4696206	TALBOT C. PTE MISSING LOCATED
	TANNER CAPT. TRANSPORT OFFICER MAYMYO TO YENANGYAUNG

4689423 TAYLORSON NAME FROM H. WEAVER
4691262 TAYLOR C. PTE MISSING LOCATED
4689570 TAYLOR "BUSTER" JACK (PONTEFRACT) CSM AT SHILLONG
4689473 TEBBETT J. PTE (BRADFORD) WOUNDED 18.2.42 SERVED IN NORWAY 1945/6
4689452 TELFORD J. CPL DIED 14.4.42
4691066 THOMAS "FREDDIE" BOY SOLDIER SURVIVED
4689700 THOMPSON G. "TOMO" PTE MISSING LOCATED DIED HEART ATTACK 1978
4688832 THOMPSON CLIFFORD SURVIVED, PIONEER SGT
4689418 THOMLINSON "TOMMO" (MERSEYSIDE) POW
4691694 THROWER H. PTE MISSING 14.4.42 NO KNOWN GRAVE
4695757 THOMPSON HAROLD PTE (SELBY) MISSING 23.2.42 NO KNOWN GRAVE
THROCKMORTON LT VERY POPULAR OFFICER
4689082 TIDSWELL R. PTE (SELBY) MISSING 19.6.42 NO KNOWN GRAVE
4689431 TIGHE BILL (NEWCASTLE) BODYGUARD TO DOYLE AND CHADWICK, CROSSED SITTANG WITH PTE TUNNEY BUT HAD TO LEAVE HIM WITH PADRE FROM WEST YORKSHIRE REG
4696252 TOWELL T. PTE DIED POW 29.12.42
4688615 TRAVIS H. PTE KILLED 10.5.42 NO KNOWN GRAVE
4690103 TROOPS R. PTE DIED 7.9.42 IN INDIA
4690511 TRYDELL W. PTE DIED POW 25.8.42
4696214 TUCKER GEORGE PTE (HULL) SWAM SITTANG TOOK SAMPAN BACK AND CAPTURED POW DIED MARCH 1990
2951343 TURNER H. PTE DIED OF WOUNDS 22.2.42 NO KNOWN GRAVE

4689633 TYLER W. CPL KILLED 28.2.42 NO KNOWN GRAVE
TYNTE R.M.H. LT/COL CAMERONIAN RIFLES TEMPERALLY IN CHARGE OF 2/KOYLI SHOT IN STOMACH BY SNIPER DIED
TUNNEY PTE CROSSED SITTANG SO EXHAUSTED HAD TO BE LEFT
ULLYATT SGT Q.M. STORES
4689039 VARLOW F. L/CPL WOUNDED
4691027 VAUSE BERNARD BOY SOLDIER (PONTEFRACT) PLAYED CLARINET LATER CHINDIT SCOUT
4690506 VOLLANS J. PTE (LEEDS) MISSING LOCATED
VALLANCE GRA LT. LATER BRIGADIER
VICKERS A.W. 2/LT STAYED AT MAYMYO
WADDINGTON L/CPL (SHEFFIELD)
WALLSTOM CPL THOUGHT MAN JUMPING OVER THE PERIMETER WALL WAS A JAP, HIT HIM FULL IN THE FACE WITH GUN BUTT, IT WAS INDIAN STRAGGLER
WALLETT PTE
4686324 WALSH T. (HUDDERSFIELD) FROM E. MUSTILL
4690288 WALTHAM J. WOUNDED – DIED 1983
4691691 WALKER W. PTE DIED POW 15.8.42
4690613 WAKE J. PTE MISSING
4694204 WALTON T. PTE KILLED 29.3.42 NO KNOWN GRAVE
WARDLEWORTH E.D. CAPTAIN SHOT IN SHOULDER SWAN SITTANG BROUGHT BOAT BACK
WARD R. PTE "BOOZER"
WATSON E.H. 2/LT DIED IN INDIA 1944
WATERS "PARNI" NAME FROM GYPO MASON
4690518 WATSON J. PTE MISSING 23.2.42 NO KNOWN GRAVE
4689170 WATSON J. PTE MISSING LOCATED
WATTS A.E. 2/LT FALL FROM HORSE BROKE COLLAR BONE NR TOKSAN

4535543 WEAVER "BUSH" HARRY CPL M.I. ROOM
WEBB S. 2/LT DIED OF WOUNDS DANYINGOI
WEEDON "TICH" C.S.M. LEG AMPUTATED
WHELLBORNE J.A. 2/LT LED ELEVEN MEN CHARGE AT TOKSAN
WHEELER T. SGT WOUNDED BILIN
4690027 WHELAN STEVE CPL (NOTTINGHAM) WOUNDED AFTER SITTANG DIED 1983
4696225 WHINCUP A.E. PTE (KNARESBOROUGH) KILLED 15.4.42 NO KNOWN GRAVE
4690613 WHITE J. PTE (LEEDS) POW SURVIVED
4688896 WHITEBROOK H."JOCK" SGT KILLED 6.6.42 ON LAST DAYS WALK OUT
4689548 WALKER ROBERT WALLIS PTE (LEEDS) SURVIVED
WHINHAM L/CPL BRIGADIERS BATMAN
4687743 WHITE H. (HUDDERSFIELD) DIED 1989
4533292 WHITFIELD S. "SHOFTI" TALLEST MAN IN BAND BIG BASS DRUM DIED 1988
4687842 WILKINS T. PTE DIED MAY 1981
4688690 WIDDOP "NUTTY" JOHN PTE WITH TED ROWLEY
4690005 WILD J.H. PTE DIED 20.3.43
4686621 WILLIAMS J. PTE MEDALS AT DONCASTER
4690822 WILLIAMS M. PTE WOUNDED
WILLIAMS "DARKY" CPL ANGLO INDIAN
4689702 WILSON E. PTE DIED 13.7.41?
4695725 WILSON HAROLD PTE (LEEDS) WOUNDED SHRAPNEL IN HIS LEG MAGWE 16.4.42
4535768 WILSON S.V. CPL DIED OF WOUNDS 19.5.42 NO KNOWN GRAVE
4689126 WILSON T. PTE DIED POW 8.3.42 NO KNOWN GRAVE
WILKINSON L/CPL NAME FROM BENNY MEE
WILSON TONY CAPTAIN DIED NEAR MAGWE

NO KNOWN GRAVE
WINCHARD CPL
4690747 WINSTANLEY E. CPL (HULL) WOUNDED WITH LT CRANFIELD NO KNOWN GRAVE
4689054 WOMACK J. SGT POW 13.3.42 COMMISSIONED K.S.L.I. DIED JUNE 1993
4690556 WOOD R.G. L/CPL (BARNSLEY) HE SHOT SNIPER, TURNED WITH THUMBS UP, ANOTHER SNIPER SHOT HIM DEAD 18.2.42 NO KNOWN GRAVE
WOOD ERNEST SGT (LEEDS) D COY
4690654 WRIGHT G. KILLED 11.5.42
WHITAKER A. 2/LT JOIN BATT, 5.3.42 AT HLEGU
WISE L.P. 2/LT JOINED BATT, 5.3.42 AT HLEGU
WATKINSON FRANK (KEIGHLEY)
WOODWARD U.G. LT (NORMANTON) EMIGRATED N/ZEALAND?
4695713 WYATT E. PTE (BARNSLEY) MISSING
4689520 YATES A.E. PTE MISSING 19.6.42 POW ESCAPED DURING LAST MONTH'S OF THE WAR WITH TED FREEMAN AND CHARLIE ACLAND SADLY DIED 4.5.1981
YATES "JOSE" JOE (FITZWILLIAM) GOOD FRIEND OF BERNARD VAUSE
4689703 YOUNG W.H. "BUNNY" PTE (LEEDS) POW SURVIVED
YOUNG A. MCL 2/LT A GOOD RELIABLE OFFICER

IT MUST BE REMEMBERED I NEVER SERVED IN BURMA AND THIS REGISTER IS MADE UP FROM VARIOUS SOURCES FROM BOOKS, REGIMENTAL HISTORY AND OFFICIAL RECORDS (THE TWO LATTER WERE NOT ALWAYS CORRECT) ALSO MAINLY FROM SURVIVORS WHO CAN BE EXCUSED IF THEIR MEMORY PLAYS TRICKS ON THEM AFTER FIFTY YEARS, OFFICIAL RECORDS WERE NOT KEPT ON A DAY TO DAY BASIS DURING THE WITHDRAWAL, FOR THE OBVIOUS REASONS THERE WAS NO TIME TO BURY THE DEAD LET ALONE KEEP RE-

CORDS OF EVERY MAN, 4689168 WILLIAM ROBINSON WAS STATED HE DIED AT PROME 4690145 WALTER POWELL WAS STATED TO HAVE BEEN KILLED HAPPILY BOTH MEN ARE STILL WITH US TODAY. YOU MAY KNOW SOMEONE'S NAME IS NOT ON THE REGISTER OR ONE OF THESE NAMED WAS NOT IN BURMA, PLEASE REMEMBER I DID MY BEST

JOHN HEALD EX 2/KOYLI

Overleaf: Two pages of Corporal Heald's Roll.

160575 FITZPATRICK GERALD 2/LT (LEEDS) JOINED BATT. HLEGU
FINNEY J. (S/LONDON) DEKHO! OBITUARY
4688434 FLEMING T CPL DIED INDIA 5·6·42
4689407 FLETCHER JAMES A. CPL (YORK) C.S.M. IN INDIA
FLETCHER FRED PTE "C" COY BROTHER TO JAMES
4696065 FLEETWOOD H. PTE MISSING 18·2·42 NO KNOWN GRAVE
2573882 FOGG S.J. PTE MISSING LOCATED LATER
4689051 FOSTER REG. L/CPL DIED A P.O.W. 19·6·44 (LEEDS)
4690347 FOWLER HARRY (HULL) DIED EARLY 1992
FOX CPL. MM, SWAM FOR ROPES TO TIE TO
DAMAGED BRIDGE STAYED IN WATER TO
HELP NON-SWIMMERS WITH L/CPL ROEBUCK
FOX C.A. CAPTAIN SUFFERED POLIO ATTACK
PUT IN CHARGE OF WIVES AND CHILDREN
FOR EVACUATION TO INDIA
FOZZARD PTE (LEEDS) HAD STALL LEEDS MARKET
FRAMTON C.Q.M.S.
4688744 FRANCE C. L/CPL MISSING 13·4·42 NO KNOWN GRAVE
4690113 FRANCE P. "FROGGY" MISSING 23·2·42 NO KNOWN GRAVE
4689490 FREEGARD C. BANDMAN DIED P.O.W.
4693834 FREEMAN TED PTE P.O.W. YENANGYAUNG ESCAPED
LAST MONTHS OF WAR DIED MORECAMBE 1993
4688658 FREEMAN SGT. WOUNDED
4687613 FRETWELL "BULL" (LEEDS) SURVIVED - MY M.T.
SGT. DEOLALI INDIA
4689767 FROST K. PTE DROWNED 23·2·42 SITTANG
RIVER NO KNOWN GRAVE
4689606 FUNK L.E. SGT. WOUNDED 23·2·42

GRACE NAME FROM BENNY MEE
4695493 GARDNER W PTE WOUNDED MISSING LOCATED
4689602 GASCOIGNE HARRY PTE (PONTEFRACT) GRAVELY
WOUNDED RESCUED BY A. MATTHEWMAN
SURVIVED LONG JOURNEY FROM SITTANG

4689520	YATES A.E. PTE MISSING 19.6.42 P.O.W. ESCAPED DURING LAST MONTH'S OF THE WAR WITH TED FREEMAN AND CHARLIE ACLAND SADLY DIED 4.5.1981
	YATES "JOSE" JOE (FITZWILLIAM) GOOD FRIEND OF BERNARD VAUSE
4689703	YOUNG W.H. "BUNNY" PTE (LEEDS) P.O.W. SURVIVED
	YOUNG A. McL. 2/LT A GOOD RELIABLE OFFICER

IT MUST BE REMEMBERED I NEVER SERVED IN BURMA AND THIS REGISTER IS MADE UP FROM VARIOUS SOURCES FROM BOOKS, REGIMENTAL HISTORY AND OFFICIAL RECORDS (THE TWO LATER WERE NOT ALWAYS CORRECT) ALSO MAINLY FROM SURVIVORS WHO CAN BE EXCUSED IF THEIR MEMORY PLAYS TRICKS ON THEM AFTER FIFTY YEARS, OFFICIAL RECORDS WERE NOT KEPT ON A DAY TO DAY BASIS DURING THE WITHDRAWAL, FOR THE OBVIOUS REASONS THERE WAS NO TIME TO BURY THE DEAD LET ALONE KEEP RECORDS OF EVERY MAN,

4689168 WILLIAM ROBINSON WAS STATED HE DIED AT PROME

4690145 WALTER POWELL WAS STATED TO HAVE BEEN KILLED HAPPILY BOTH MEN ARE STILL WITH US TO DAY.

YOU MAY KNOW SOMEONE'S NAME IS NOT ON THE REGISTER OR ONE OF THESE NAMED WAS NOT IN BURMA, PLEASE REMEMBER I DID MY BEST JOHN HEALD EX 2/KOYLI

Appendix E

Reliability of memory and the experience of warfare

The following are some of the conclusions drawn by Ralph Tanner after being the subject of research into memory by three eminent psychologists on the fallibility of memory, and those of David Tanner on the reliability of documents as an historical resource. Ralph is an active social scientist with a substantial corpus of published work, so his reflections come with some authority. His full analysis of the experience was published by Kluwer Academic Publishers in 2001. This Appendix is not an essential adjunct to the foregoing narrative, but it may be of interest both to those have their own memories of warfare and to those who wish to record, organise and publicise those memories – the historians.

Even for the professional soldier the experience of war is one of peaks of fear or excitement and long periods of inactivity. Faced with a request for information that happened long ago the result is going to be a patchwork of questionable accuracy and perhaps of limited interest to people who are not close to the person remembering, or who did not share in his or her experiences. 'Reliability is, in general, inversely proportional to the time lapse between the event and the recollection.' (Gottschalk 1945.)

The challenge for historians is, what is correct, and is it ever possible to discern the truth of a certain event? While a military document may seem to be an accurate record of events, war diaries of units are almost invariably written up after the events they record and are subject to considerable editing to avoid recording discreditable behaviour. A written order is a self-evident truth but a week later the memory of that order – how it was delivered and how received – is fading. Military records relating to actions are sparsely distributed and retained depending on whether the military units are advancing or retiring and whether such records survive the uncertainties of warfare – rain, fire and the practicalities of keeping out-of-date communications when mules are the only means of transport. The Imperial War Museum contains very little documentation related to the battle of Crete or the epic retreat from Burma except high level situation reports and telegrams.

Ralph Tanner asked military records for details of his six years of army service and received some two hundred pages of bureaucratic data about his movements, medical boards and promotions. It recorded that he had been a member of a specially trained anti-tank squad in 1940, which is an elaboration from a single exercise in which some training was given in the use of Molotov cocktails. It was startling to discover that there was nothing providing any evidence that he had ever been in action and there was nothing in this mass of documents recording that he had been Mentioned in Despatches. So the written records which survive are not likely always to disclose much that is of interest to the historian in the reconstruction of events, nor would they necessarily have any bearing on reality

The accuracy and inaccuracy of recalled memories may be quite unintentional or involve deliberate or unconscious deception. The traumatic nature of many war memories means that they may require substantial editing before an individual is prepared to divulge them to others. The difficulty here is that as any war becomes more and more a part of history the amount of written material available for study and interpretation is unlikely to increase except for the appearance of diaries, which are intrinsically personal creations. This then becomes 'mutilated knowledge' (Veyne 1984). The main source of data may become the personal reminiscences of those involved and over time the possibility of being able to assert their accuracy by triangulation with other data become more difficult.

There are occasional opportunities to prove or disprove a memory. Ralph Tanner remembers an event in Crete May 1941 in which he was asked by Col Laycock commanding the Commando Layforce whether he knew how to fire a Vickers machine-gun to cover a track near a chapel. He visited the place thirty years later and found that the chapel faced the opposite direction to the one he remembered, and that the hills he remembered on the east of the track were on the west. Without any doubt the memory was wrong, showing that an incorrect memory can survive over a considerable time. There was nothing in this event that might have prompted the creation and maintenance of a false memory; it was not, for example, recording a violent incident, or cowardice, or bravery. It was just one event in a traumatic week.

Ralph's first job on being commissioned in Burma in January 1942 was to escort the Battalion's wives and children from Maymyo, with a night at Yenangyaung, to the airfield at Magwe for evacuation by air to India. While writing this book he met a man who, as a boy, had been in that convoy. He stated that they had spent the night at Mandalay and not at Yenangyaung as Ralph Tanner had recorded and remembered. As this was the first occasion that this nine-year-old boy had had his life so radically disturbed, his memories might well have been more accurate than those of a young officer about to experience the traumatic events of the retreat soon afterwards.

These two flat contradictions of the author's recollections should be a warning to all who take the recorded memories of ex-combatants as facts. There is always a need for a caveat.

It would seem that the nearer to the events such memories are the greater the likelihood of their accuracy and as discussed the greater the distance in time the greater the opportunity for inaccuracy. Some reminiscences of Battalion personnel describe with great vividness events some thirty years later, but we have every reason to entertain doubts as to their accuracy.

The greater the level of literacy the greater the requirement to remember hard data; however, the counter to this is that because of the availability of hard data in print, modern societies tend to have to remember less. Thus there is a danger of memory being 'attuned to' the availability of reference data. This becomes a false memory or 'mutilated knowledge'.

There have been substantial efforts to find out experimentally what people remember and how memory changes over time and for what reasons. These experiments take the individual out of the ongoing social environment in which such memories were created and kept in the mind. Such experiments are isolated from the environment of warfare; the sound, sickness, the smell of the dead and the wonderful taste of food and drink that would be rejected in a peacetime café. These experiments remain what they are, rather special social activities, which have little relationship to the wider social environment and they are not by definition a slice out of a past life. When the author was the subject of the unusual experiment in memory in relation to his unread diary mentioned in the introduction to this Appendix, this prolonged experiment on an articulate individual with an academic background suggested that memory was a kind of social tool. We do not know what is remembered unless it has been, as it were, pulled out of retirement by some external event, or because the subject is asked questions about his experiences, or volunteers to provide them. In the former case, the sound of a Bofors gun in an old news reel, the author's mental agitation in going past HMS *Belfast* moored near the Tower of London because he had sailed in HMS *Abdiel* and HMS *Isis* during the Crete campaign, or a swish of sound from some source evoking the memory of an incoming mortar shell, are all examples.

It seems clear that the brain does not necessarily retain a record of everything that it has experienced; it must cast away information as new stimuli come in. Much is too commonplace to be retained – meals, washing and marching – of which little will be recorded. However, it seems that virtually anything can be brought out when it has the appropriate stimuli. The subconscious is not necessarily going to remember what interested outsiders might consider to be important events. The author remembers humming the theme from a pre-war musical sung by Gertrude Lawrence that he had not even seen while in a ditch under shell fire near Magwe. Even a week after a military action it seems unlikely that those involved would be able to produce a coherent account of their own activities that would clearly coincide with the memories of others.

What is remembered and why? The Japanese records show that there had been hard fighting at Migyaungye where they had 23 men killed. Although Ralph Tanner was only a short distance from this fighting the diary does not record any details or indeed that there had been any fighting of such intensity. Perhaps there is a circle of awareness outside of which there is no reason to record anything, particularly in stressful situations. On the same day the diary records the author being warned that there were Japanese by a tree a hundred yards ahead of where he was lying. Certainly a frightening event, but he has no recollection of it at all.

So what is remembered may be distributed between what the conscious mind wishes to remember, as it is important at that time, and what the subconscious may decide should be remembered. The mind will always be reacting to fit in with the roles that the individual is currently performing; that of ex-soldier may well have a lower priority than the memory needs of father, husband or friend. The memory of even specific events may be constantly adjusting according to the up-to-date social and psychological needs of an individual.

Why should memories of past events, however traumatic they may have been, be expected to be both static and accurate when every other human characteristic is changing under new social experiences and the natural processes of ageing? Memories of what has been experienced can be expected to move with the times. It would be wrong surely to see these changes as passively occurring. This is an active process. What may have happened in a distant war can be way down the list of psychological needs. It would be prudent to see any part of a memory as responding to variations in a hierarchy of those conscious and unconscious needs. The fact that the records of an individual show minor contradictions is as much evidence of their overall accuracy as inaccuracy: it is some kind of evidence of an editing process.

Moral judgement plays a part in this. An ex-soldier may be aware that his behaviour as well as that of others may on occasions have been poor and thus best omitted or disguised in memory. It is reasonable to discuss the awful behaviour of British soldiers at the sacking of Badajoz in the Peninsular War but not for any possible comparable behaviour in recent wars when their relatives are still alive. Any regimental history may well miss the recording of much reality. through such censorship, as may the subconscious of an individual. Malice may even shape or distort the memories of the less successful survivors of warfare.

Memories of warfare have to be judiciously interpreted with as much triangulation as is available from any historical resource. These memories are individual pictures of the past that can be meaningfully compared with paintings or poetry. They are personal creations. This is why Ralph Tanner's diary and notes and John Heald's hand-written roll have been reproduced here exactly as they were produced by them. There has been no editing, and the inconsistencies, where evident, have been highlighted and in fact add veracity to the record of events as Ralph saw them.

Notes

1. Lowenthal. 1997. Quoting the first line of L.P. Hartley's *The Go-Between*, 1953.
2. Produced by Lt. Col. Chadwick in discussion with other survivors at Shillong in mid-1942.
3. Recalled by Ralph Tanner, but no evidence can be located.
4. Throckmorton, Major and Anne, Capt. (1943). Story of the 2/ KOYLI from leaving Yenangyaung on 11 April 1942 until arriving at Imphal, Assam. Typed. In Regimental Records. Light Infantry Yorkshire Depot, Pontefract.
5. Privately printed in Tokyo in Japanese.
6. The Japanese local government structure equivalent of a British county.
7. 2/Lieut Geoffrey Cranfield, 217668 was killed in action on 14 April 1942. Commonwealth War Graves Commission records.
8. Grant, I.L. and Tamayama, K. (1999). *Burma. 1942: The Japanese Invasion*, Appendix 9. Zampi, Chichester.
9. Records of the USAAF (http://www.usaaf.net/chron/42/mar42.htm, and also edited by Jack Killop USAF) state that the evacuation occurred between 8–13 March when 474 troops and 29 tons of supplies were flown in and 423 civilians evacuated using 8 B17s flying in and out of Magwe.
10. 2nd. Lieut. James Ableson, 77920, was killed in action on 8 March 1942. Commonwealth War Graves Commission records.
11. This incident is not mentioned in the diary itself, only in a later addition.
12. Lieut. M. Phillips, 104934, died on 19 April 1942. Commonwealth War Graves Commission records.
13. Cede nullis is the Regimental motto of the Kings Own Light Infantry.

14. Capt. Robinson, ex 11 Scottish Commando. After the disbandment of the Middle East Commandos, Evelyn Waugh returned to the UK. At that time he offered to arrange for Ralph Tanner to become a Cipher Sergeant in Cairo but Ralph did not like the idea, as based at Geneifa in the Canal Zone he would have been sent to the infantry pool for the Middle East and ended up in the desert. Robinson, an Englishmen in Scottish Commando 11, was taking a small draft of 20-plus men to join Mission 204 in Burma. Tanner volunteered to be his batman and that is how he learnt to iron tartan trews and kilts. They travelled on the SS *Queen Elizabeth* from Suez to Trincomalee in Sri Lanka, by train to Calcutta, by cargo boat to Rangoon and then train to Maymyo. Mission 204 was aimed at giving guerrilla training to the Chinese, so they trained with a light machine gun, not the Bren, and used Chinese maps. For fear of alerting the Japanese it was called the Bush Warfare School, in which there was an Australian contingent. Much has been published on their fruitless activities. Ralph thinks he must have met Robinson again after they had been flown out of China, since he recalls an anecdote regarding Robinson's lunch with Wavell in Delhi; the conversation was all provided by Lady Wavell, as Wavell himself said nothing.
15. This camera was later exchanged for one that was used by Ralph Tanner on the retreat. It therefore seems likely that the shotgun reference in the Diary should be read as a .22 rifle.
16. 'in little room off entrance' seems to have been added at a later date.
17. Records of the USAAF (http://www.usaaf.net/chron/42/mar42.htm, and also edited by Jack Killop USAF) confirm this and state that the evacuation occurred between 8–13 March, when 474 troops and 29 tons of supplies were flown in and 423 civilians evacuated using eight B17s flying in and out of Magwe.
18. This comment was added in the period 1945–6 when Ralph Tanner was resident in Lashio as evidenced by his use of yellow US Army message paper which was abundant in Lashio at that time.
19. See note 18.

20. This is assumed to be Major David Martin, the Adjutant of 2Bn KOYLI, after whom David Tanner is named.
21. The Thompson submachine gun was not standard issue to the 2Bn KOYLI. It was however issued to FF7, a BFF (Burma Frontier Force) unit formed in late January 1942 to help in the protection of Burmese oil facilities. This issue was one TSMG per section, 'but not a single round of ammunition' (Braund 1972: 154) and FF7 was withdrawn from Syriam between 7–11 March. Rangoon fell on 9 March. Braund reported that the BFF fought at Yenangyaung. The Yenangyaung oil facility was destroyed on 15 April. It seems likely that Ralph Tanner acquired his weapon from the BFF or from their abandoned facilities, or from the Nationalist Chinese forces who were also issued with Thompsons, given the cooperative nature of the ground conflict at this juncture in the campaign. The only weapon of this type in use at this time was the .45 calibre M1928 with a drum magazine. This is confirmed by the 3 May diary entry.
22. This aircraft was almost certainly the Mitsubishi Ki-51 officially designated the Army Type 99 Assault Plane, code-named 'Sonia' by the Allies. Designed to meet the Japanese Army requirement of a ground-attack aircraft in 1937, this aircraft saw service first in China and then throughout the Pacific War.
23. It seems unlikely that Ralph Tanner would have carried a .45 TMSG, a .303 Enfield and have had the standard .38 side arm of an officer. It seems likely therefore that the rifle mentioned referred to his TSMG, as there are only two references to a rifle in his diary. There is however mention in Appendix A/2 of owning a .22 rifle when still a Private with Mission 204 in Maymyo.
24. Ralph Tanner was with a 'guide', presumably Burmese as a British soldier would not have adequate local knowledge, so the request must have been translated.
25. Were there two white soldiers and a guide or was the 'guide' in fact a soldier who had recently covered the territory?
26. The only Bootland death recorded by the CWGC in Burma in 1942 was that of Pvte. R. S. Bootland, 4536784 of the West Yorkshire Regiment (Prince of Wales's Own) on 30 March 1942.

27. Latimer refers to this stream as Pin Chaung.
28. This is the only mention of a shotgun and it might refer to the .22 rifle acquired when still a Private in Mission 204 in Maymyo.
29. This is likely to have been Major David Martin.
30. Lieut. M Phillips, 104934, died on 19 April 1942. Commonwealth War Graves Commission records.
31. Latimer page 458 refers to the death of Mrs Waddleworth at Myitkyina in a strafed Dakota on which she was trying to escape with other evacuees. At this point Waddleworth cannot have known of his wife's death.
32. This comment was added in the period 1944–5 when Ralph Tanner was resident in Lashio as evidenced by his use of yellow US Army message paper, which was abundant in Lashio at that time.
33. This comment was added later on a scrap of torn white paper and like all other notes attached to the diary with a pin.
34. Written in pencil. The diary was written in ink.
35. Ralph Tanner is most probably referring to Thaungtha.
36. This comment was added in the period 1944–5 when Ralph Tanner was resident in Lashio as evidenced by his use of yellow US Army message paper, which was abundant in Lashio at that time.
37. Major David E Martin 73664, aged 24 died from his wounds suffered in the demolition of stores kept in the cinema in Yenangyuang on 7 May 1942. Commonwealth war graves commission records, and Ralph Tanner recollections.
38. Photograph number 15.
39. This comment was added in the period 1944–5 when Ralph Tanner was resident in Lashio as evidenced by his use of white US Army message paper, which was abundant in Lashio at that time.
40. See note 39.
41. See note 39.
42. This must refer to a photograph of which there is no trace.
43. See note 39.
44. This comment was written later on a scrap of torn white paper and like all other notes attached to the diary with a pin.

45. See note 39.
46. These last two sentences are written with a different pen to the main diary and demonstrate a greater lucidity than other entries, suggesting that they were written much later when there had been time for reflection.
47. See note 39.

Bibliography

Akert, R.M. (1993). 'The effect of autobiographical memories on the current definition of self'. Unpublished mss. Wellesley College.

Allen, L. (1984). *Burma: The Longest War*, Dent, London.

Baddeley, A.D. (1972). 'Selective attention and performance in dangerous environments'. *British Journal of Psychology*. 63:537–546.

Bayley, C. and Harper, T. (2005). *Forgotten Armies*, Penguin, London.

Baxter, W, (1955). *Look down in Mercy*, Heinemann, London.

Beevor, A. (1991). *Crete: The Battle and the Resistance*, Murray, London.

Belden, J. (1943). *Retreat with Stilwell*, Cassell, London.

Carew, T. (1969). *The Longest Retreat*, Hamilton, London.

Carmichael, P. (1983). *Mountain Battery*, Devin, Bournemouth.

Clifford, B.R. and Scott, J. (1978). 'Individual and situational factors in eye-witness testimony', *Journal of Applied Psychology* 63:352–359.

Clifford, F. (1960). *A Battle is Fought to be Won*, Hamilton, London.

Colvin, J. (1994). *Not Ordinary Men. The Battle of Kohima Reassessed*, Cooper, London.

Cooper, K.W. (1973). *The Little Men. A Platoon's Epic Fight in the Burma Campaign*, Hale, London.

Edwards, L, (2009). *Kohima: The Furthest Battle*, The History Press, Stroud.

Fergusson, B. (1946). *The Wild Green Earth*, Collins, London.

Fitzpatrick, G. (2001). *No Mandalay. No Maymyo (79 survived)*, Book Guild, Lewes.

Fraser, G.M. (1992). *Quartered Safe out Here. A Recollection of the War in Burma*, Harvill, London.

Gottschalk, L. (1945). *The Use of Personal Documents in History,* New York Social Science Council, New York.

Grant, I.L. and Tamayama, K. (1999). *Burma 1942: The Japanese Invasion*, Zampi, Chichester.

Hamilton, I (1910). *Staff Officers Scrap Book during the Russo-Japanese War*, Arnold, London.

Hilgard, E.R. et al. (1975). *Introduction to Psychology*, Harcourt, Bruce Jovanovich, New York.

Hingston, W. (1950). *History of the King's Own Yorkshire Light Infantry*, Volume V. Lund Humphries, London. 143–234.

Howarth, K. (1999). *Oral history: A Handbook*, Sutton, Stroud.

Iida, Shojiro. (1990). *Senjin Yawa* (Stories from the battlefields).

Kinchin, D. (2004). *Post Traumatic Stress Disorder: The Invisible Injury*, Success, Didcot.

Latimer, J. (2004). *The Forgotten War*, Murray, London.

Loftus, E.F. (1996). *Eyewitness Testimony*, Harvard University Press, Cambridge, Mass.

Lone, S. (1998). *The Japanese military during the Russo-Japanese war 1904–5. A reconsideration of command politics and public images*, London School of Economics, University of London.

Lowenthal, D. (1997). *The Past is a Foreign Country*, Cambridge University Press, Cambridge.

Lunt, J. (1986) *A Hell of a Licking*, Collins, London.

Morison, S.A. (1950), 'Breaking the Bismarck Barrier', *History of US Naval Operations in World War Two*, Volume 6:186. Little Brown, Boston.

Randle, J. (2005). *Battle Tales from Burma*, Pen and Sword, Barnsley.

Slim, W. (1956). *Defeat into Victory*, Cassell, London.

Smyth, J (1979). *Milestones,* Sidgwick & Jackson, London.

Veyne, P. (1984). *Writing History*, Manchester University Press, Manchester.

Waugh, E (1976). *The Diaries of Evelyn Waugh*, Weidenfeld & Nicholson, London.

Ward, M.C. (1997). 'The European method of warring is not practised here: The failure of British military policy in the Ohio valley 1755–1759'. *War in History*. 4(3):247–263.

Weinstein, N.D. (1960). 'Unrealistic optimism about future life events', *Journal of Personality and Social Psychology* 39:806–820

Index

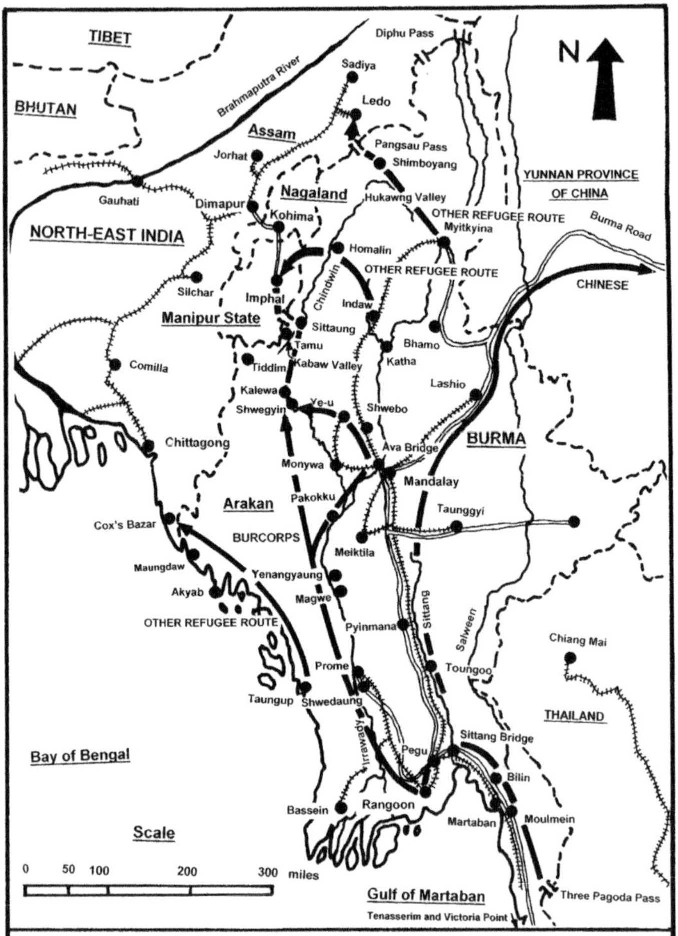

ALLIED AND REFUGEE RETREAT ROUTES FOLLOWING JAPANESE INVASION

Maps courtesy of Leslie Edwards, from *Kohima: The Furthest Battle*, published by The History Press.

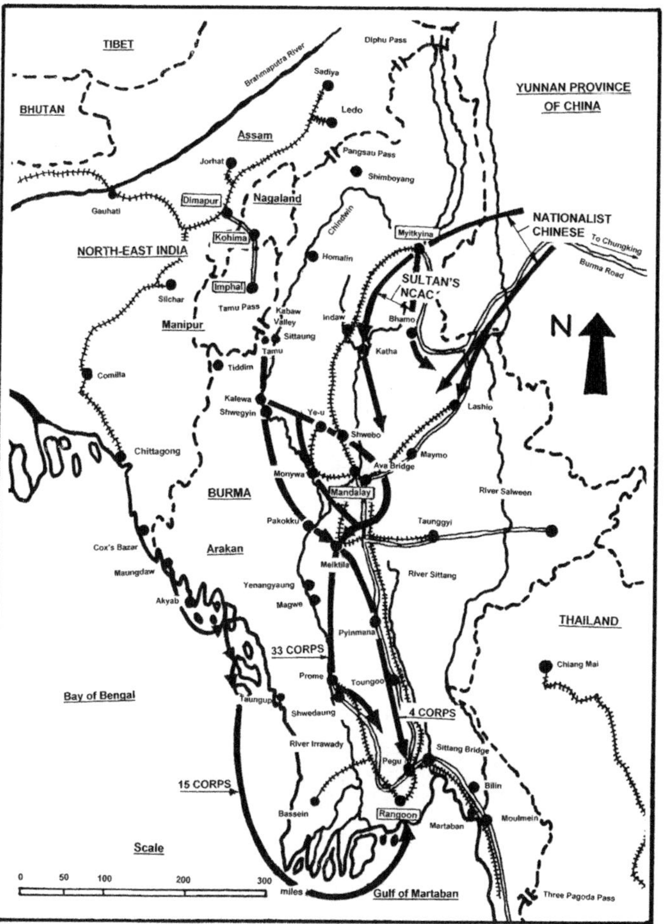

ALLIED RECAPTURE OF BURMA

Some went back.

Also from The History Press ...

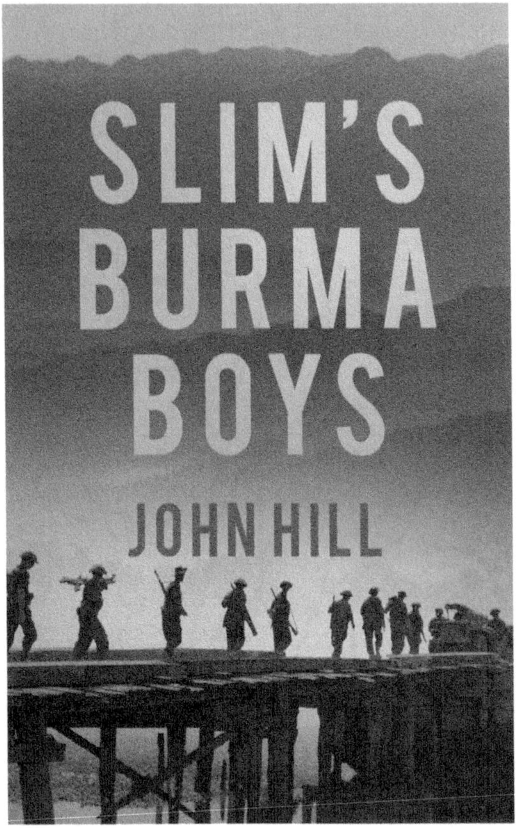

9780750992060